PAIN INTO PURPOSE

Battling Grief through the eyes of HER...

An Inspirational Memoir

Tanika K. Judie

PAIN INTOPURPOSE:

Battling Greif through the eyes of HER...

An Inspirational Memoir

By Tanika Judie

Authors Bio:

Tanika K. Judie is an amazing 33-year-old woman of God who takes pride in helping others. While rebuilding her life in Kansas City Missouri (KCMO) and taking care of her four children she manages to work a full-time job, write, speak and find time to encourage and uplift as many people as she can. Tanika has been writing in journals and speaking publicly since she was a young girl. She takes pride in her ability to connect with others through her trails, joys, testimonies, spiritual gifts and through her smile. Her personality will light up a room and have you laughing as she is a joy to have around with her "No sad faces attitude." After finally being obedient to God she wrote and published her first book and is currently working on the second one. She hopes to encourage and impact the world with her life story but more than anything else her hope is that the people who read her books turn to God and he gets all the glory!

While going through a difficult time in her life, she felt the need to journal her experiences and share with her audiences the unfiltered parts of her journey and she believes it is a good way to heal. She challenges you to do the same.

DEDACATION

This book is dedicated to my love, my fiancé Dorron L. Blackmon. You inspired me to pursue my dreams no matter what and I'm doing just that. Rest in Heaven my Buddy! To my children; Ar'Terion, Aerin, Anton and Alece. You guys have not only been what keeps me going day to day but you guys are the reason I get up and fight for my life. I look at you guys and you give me a reason to live! To God for having favor over my life and loving me more then I love myself, for carrying me when I couldn't move at all and for giving me the courge to speak about it. This book is also dedicated to anyone who has ever experienced pain of any kind, heart break, depression and for those who have ever felt like giving up. God loves you and I pray that this book helps you.

TABLE OF CONTENTS

This is a true story, but I have changed the names of all the people in my story. However, all details of my story are true based on my recollection of the events that occurred.

PROLOGUE

March 11, 2017

Ring . . . Ring . . . I roll over and glimpse at the cell phone, thinking it's Ah'Lee calling me back. But as my eyes adjust, I see that the phone reads, Johnson Sister, Tasha. Searching my mind for why she might be calling, I quickly push the side button to stop the ringing, knowing it will go to voicemail, and then I see the time: 2:30 a.m.

"What could she possibly want this early in the morning?" my mind reels, pushing me more fully awake, but then I quickly realize, "Maybe she's trying to see if her brothers with me."

Rolling back over, I adjust my pillow, attempting to slip back into sleep. Just as I close my eyes, the mood is broken with another ring. Quickly glancing up, I see that it's her again! For a split second I want to push the side button, but then decide I should probably answer—it's not like her to call in the middle of the night.

"Hello?" I rasp, trying not to sound alarmed.

"Tamika?"

"Yeah, what's up Tasha?"

Then instantly, her next words made my heart drop into my gut, taking my breath away.

"Ah'Lee got shot!"

I jump up in a panic, barely able to breathe. "WHAT? Wait, he got shot, is he okay!?"

Through tears, the story spills out . . . "Somebody tried to rob him, Tamika . . . and they shot him!"

"Tasha, is he okay?" I ask again, trying to stay calm. "Where did he get shot?"

"In the leg," she says.

I swallow hard. "What part of his leg?"

From attending nursing school in the past and losing a friend to a gunshot wound to the leg, I know that there's a main artery in your leg that can cause you to bleed out in seconds.

"I don't know," Tasha sobs, "but they said he kept blacking out."

"No! I'm on my way," I say, "but . . . I'm in Texas."

When she tells me he's been blacking out, I know the bullet must have hit his artery. I hang up the phone and wake up my kids in a panic.

"GET UP, GET UP, WE HAVE TO GO!!!" I shake them all awake.

Sleep talking, they ask, "Why, mama?" At that moment my stomach feels empty and a burning knot is stuck in my throat as I try to pull out the words, conveying the one thing I've always dreaded . . .

"Ah'Lee got shot!!" I finally say, my voice now shaking.

My children began to ask questions. "Is he okay?"

The twins ask, "Mama, is Daddy okay?

I look at them with tear-filled eyes and trying to remain calm, I stammer, "I think so. We just have to get to him because he's waiting for us."

While the kids get dressed, I started packing our belongings; I feel as if time has stopped and I'm moving in slow motion. I can feel my heart beating through my chest, much slower than normal. I can't breathe very well but hear every shallow, labored breath.

Then suddenly, something tells me to stop and pray. I immediately stop, gathered my kids around me and held their hands. Then the words come tumbling out . . . the words I will soon regret praying. I know I will never forget this moment, this feeling, this deep angst . . . and will keep it in my heart forever.

"Dear God," I begin, "I come to you now, asking you to protect Ah'Lee. I ask that you keep him safe. I ask that you allow us to get home safely. Lord, I ask that you let your will be done in this situation. In Jesus name, we pray, Amen!"

The kids say, "Amen," and we grab their things and scramble out the hotel door. Feeling like I'm in a dream, I stopped at the desk to let them know I was checking out early. My clarity of mind surprises me. Yet opening the car door, I can't stop shaking and thinking about Ah'Lee. So many thoughts, fears, and hopes begin swirling in my head.

Is he going to be okay? Is he up waiting on me? Is he looking for me? Is he thinking about me? Why did I leave? I need to be there by his side. Why am I not there when he needs me the most?

I'm a wreck. Not knowing what to do, I'm in a panic, trying to think of some way I can get home faster than the seven hours it took me to get to Texas from Missouri. While wracking my brain, I'm also thinking about who I can ask to go to the hospital to let Ah'Lee know I'm on my way and to wait on me. Every 30 minutes I try calling his phone, but it always goes straight to voicemail, fraying my nerves still more. My thoughts are frenzied. I simply must find someone to go talk to him and check on him!

I call my sister, Tisha. When she answers, I try my best to stay calm and tell her what happened. After managing to get it out, I ask, "Will you please go to the hospital and make sure he's okay and let him know I'm on my way?"

"Yes, yes, try to calm down," Tisha reassures me. "I'm going up there—I don't want you to get sick while you're on the road."

"Okay, thank you!" and we hang up the phone.

The next chain of events changes the lives of my children and me forever!

◆ ◆ ◆

You see, in that fragile, precarious moment in time, my fiancé, my best-friend, my lover, my partner, my teammate, my biggest supporter . . . left me!!

However, before I can tell you how my pain turns into purpose, I have to give you the back story—so here it is.

1. HOW WE MET

May 2011

I must tell you the story as I remember it.

First, my cousins, sister, and I were at a club, in Kansas City, Missouri (and not too far from where I lived off 16th and Jackson). We left the club, maybe around 2:30 a.m., but then agreed we still wanted to hang out. Knowing the best late-night party spot we arrived at a small place that was always crowded (an after-hours club on 31st and Prospect, in KCMO). I remember drinking more and dancing a lot—my favorite thing those days. After an hour or so, I needed a break and ended up sitting down at a table close to the entrance. Sitting there, we continued to drink and talk about our night.

Just then I looked up and saw him . . . and I couldn't stop staring.

He was sexy, dark-skinned, with a medium build and an even cut, not low but not too high. He had chestnut color eyes and, to top it off, he was wearing my favorite color, black. He had on a black shirt, black shorts, and some all-black Jordan's.

My eyes kept staring at him, walking in like he owned the place. Not in an arrogant way but with an air of confidence. He ambled past me, all the way to the back of the club. Turning around close to the wall, he put his hands behind his back and skimmed the place, checking his surroundings but never speaking a word. A few people walked up, shook his hand, and then walked off. But he never moved.

It was like he came just for me—that's all I could think of. I don't know what it was about this sexy, black man, but it was something that kept me completely focused on him. I literally couldn't take my eyes off him. He didn't do anything special but just stood there, observing everyone. No, we never made eye contact, but I knew I wanted him. And I was determined to get him.

That's one thing about me: if I want something, I go for it, with no hesitation. It was something about his smooth, dark skin and confidence that made him stand out from the rest. It was crazy, but I remember looking at my cousin, asking, "Dana, who is that?"

She looked at me, smiling, and said, "That's Bread Bread. He be next door to my momma's house from time to time. He hella cool and laid back."

I said, "Aw yeah, I want him, cousin. I gotta have him."

After that, I continued to watch him, making a mental note that before either one of us left that after-hours, I was going to say something to him. I watched him a bit longer, just kind of sizing him up. But the crazy thing is, as I was looking at him, it was like everybody else just disappeared. No lie . . . it was like off a movie. All I saw was him.

I shook my head and said, "Dang, that's him." I got up and danced a little more but kept watching him closely. He spoke to a couple more people when they approached him, but he just kept standing there. After about an hour, I saw him heading for the door—and I knew I had to make my move. I said to myself. "I'm about to get him." I walked over to him, trying to sound and look as sober as I could, and began to speak.

"Excuse me."

He looked back and turned around to face me.

He said, "What's up?"

I said, "Hey, my name is Tamika. What's your name?"

He smiled, showing his even, perfect teeth and said, "Bread." When he smiled, I lost myself for a second because his smile was so pretty.

I looked him in his eyes and said, "No, what's your name, because I know yo momma didn't name you Bread." I gave you my government name, so now I want yours—'cause I want to know *you*, not you as Bread."

He smiled again, saying, "My name is Ah'Lee."

I stretched my hand out to shake his hand and said, "Nice to meet you, Ah'Lee." At that point, I felt like a Lady Mac and smiled at him with the sexiest smile I could.

He shook my hand and said, "Put my number in yo phone." I did as he told me, and I gave him my number too. He locked the number in and said, "Call me when you get home."

I looked at him puzzled and thought to myself, *"What does he think is about to happen tonight, 'cause he ain't getting none of this."* However, I kept my composure and said, "Okay, I will."

He said, "Cool," and turned and walked out of the after-hours. I went back to my cousin, told her about our conversation and said, "I got him." We both laughed and continued our night.

Around 4:45 or 5:00 a.m., I made it home, sat on my bed, and my first thought was of this sexy chocolate man I had just met.

I was like, should I call him. I said to myself, *"Yeah,"* then I was like *"No, you're tripping—ain't nothing open but legs."* Then against my better judgment, I called him.

I dialed the number, and after two rings, he picked up. "Hello."

I said (trying not to sound nervous), "Hey, Ah'Lee, this is Tamika. You told me to call you when I got home, so I called."

He said, "That's what's up . . . I just wanted to make sure you got home safe."

I pulled the phone back, looked at it, and thought to myself, *"What? This thug's got a heart."* I put the phone back to my ear and said, "Yeah, I did. Well, goodnight."

He said, "Goodnight. I'll call you in the morning."

I said, "Okay," and we hung up the phone.

I set the phone down on the bed and smiled, saying out loud, "He's the one."

From that day on, Ah'Lee and I kept in contact. I told him I was a single mother of four—two boys and two girls. I shared with Ah'Lee about the passing of their fathers, which left me alone to take care of my children. Ah'Lee told me that God had me, and He did too. . . that was a statement He definitely lived up to. Ah'Lee also told me about his daughter, whom he hadn't seen in about a year, if I'm not mistaken, and why he hadn't seen her. We talked mainly over the phone in the beginning because he was going back in forth between Missouri and Columbia, which was almost two hours away. We didn't get to see each other as much face to face, but it was cool because it made our conversations good.

At the time, I never asked why he went to Columbia so much, but later found out that he had family there. Then one day I pulled up to a store to see him. It was called, The Spot, on 35th and Troost. I got out of my car, gave him a hug, and we had a brief conversation. Due to the location of the store, we didn't stay long at all, but to me, it was long enough because I got to see him. After we hooked up that day, we started talking even more on the phone.

After getting to know him, I found that he was a humble and cool guy. Ah'Lee told me about his most recent relationship, and I told him about mine. We both decided we would take it slow and see what happened, and that's just what we did. I felt like Ah'Lee was "the one"—he made me so happy whenever we talked. He was just so sweet to me. As time went by, he started coming to see me more.

Then all of a sudden, after nine or ten months, he disappeared.

His phone was going to voicemail when I called, and I couldn't get in touch with him. *"Dang, did I do something?"* I was upset that he just left without an explanation and worried about him all at the same time. That was because, after getting to know him, I found that he made a lot of "runs." He wasn't a bad guy; he just got money the best way he could to take care of his family.

After about two weeks of looking for him and still nothing, I said to myself, *"Maybe he's done."* I stopped calling his phone because it wasn't getting me anywhere, but I thought about him a lot.

While getting to know Ah'Lee, I found that he was really quiet and laid back. He wasn't much of a talker unless he was drinking, which wasn't often because he smoked more than anything. I missed Ah'Lee but had to continue my life. Then a month passed, and I still didn't hear from him.

2. THE REUNION

May 26, 2012

It was late in the day and I was bored, wanting to get out of the house. It felt good outside, so I called my sister and asked her what she was doing. She said she was going to GQ's on 47th in Prospect—to a motorcycle party—and said I should come up there too.

I told her, "Cool, I'm coming." So, after hopping in the shower, I threw on something simple: a colorful romper with some coach shoes that matched perfectly. I straightened my hair and put on a brown and tan headband. I accessorized, of course, and made sure I was all lotioned up. The shoes I wore showed my toes, so thank God they were freshly done with French tips that matched my nails. I looked in the mirror to make sure I was ready and headed out the door.

I pulled up to the club, and man, it was jumping. There were motorcycles and people with their vests on, standing in front of the club. I called my sister to make sure she was there. After the first ring, she answered, saying she was on her way to the door to meet me. I stepped out of my champagne-colored, four-door, 2005 Pontiac Grand Prix and walked across the street to the front of the club. My sister walked out and saw me, and we went straight in, eventually sitting down to have drinks with her friends. We danced and chilled. I remember sitting close to the door and the dance floor. My sister was a two-stepper, and I loved to see her dance, so I just sat there for a couple of hours, watching her and enjoying the music.

After a while we decided we needed to step outside for

some air, so we sat outside and chilled some more. It was just that kind of night! My sister smoked a cigarette and shared laughs with her friends. I stood off to the side, looking around at the people but not really recognizing anyone. Looking over to my left, I spotted one of my old friends: a dude I'd known since I was 15 years old. I called his name, and he turned around ... and when he did there was a dude standing to his left who looked very familiar. So, I walked a little closer—and that's when I saw him.

I said to myself, "That's Ah'Lee!" I was super happy but didn't want to seem desperate—so I waited on our mutual friend to walk over to me. When he got closer, we embraced and had a short conversation, just kind of catching up. At the end of our conversation, I asked him to tell his friend to come here.

He said, "Who, Bread Bread?"

I said, "Yeah, I been looking for him."

He laughed and said, "Okay," and walked back to Ah'Lee.

I saw the two of them talking, looking in my direction, and then Ah'Lee smiled and came my way. When Ah'Lee approached me, I smiled and asked, "Do you remember me?"

He smiled and said, "Yeah."

I asked, "Well, what's my name?"

He looked at me with those chestnut eyes and said, "Tamika," smiling that beautiful smile. Once again, his smile put me in a daze, and I had to pull myself together.

I said, "Where you been? I have been looking for you."

He said, "I was in jail." Then he explained. "After seeing' you last, I had to go to court, and they took me to jail over some warrant they said I had." Ah'Lee proceeded to tell me that he couldn't remember my number, so he couldn't call me.

"Cool ... well, I'm glad you're good, I was worried."

Ah'Lee stepped back and just looked at me from head to toe, but he didn't say a word. He got down to my feet and stared at them for what felt like forever. I got really uncomfortable and said, "What are you looking at?"

He said, "Your feet."

I asked, "Why?" and cocked my head to the side, very confused.

He looked up at me and said, "Because I have to make sure my girl has pretty feet," and smiled.

"Well, did I pass the test?" I asked, giving him a smile right back.

He said, "Yeah," and we both laughed. Until this day, nobody can tell me my feet are ugly because Ah'Lee said they were cute.

From that day on, Ah'Lee and I saw each other almost every day. We talked about a lot of things and got to know each other better.

◆ ◆ ◆

On June 26, Ah'Lee and I were together and went to get a room. I remember it like it was yesterday because it was the birthday of one of my best friends, and Young Jeezy came to KC for a concert. Well, long story short, Ah'Lee and I shared something we had never talked about. I felt as if I had to tell him this because this was the first time we stayed together overnight. I told Ah'Lee I had Epilepsy. He asked me what that was. I explained that it means a person has seizures that come from the brain. I told Ah'Lee what to do just in case I had one when we were together. And he took it like it was nothing.

He then said he was a Diabetic and that he takes pills every day. Then he told me not only the story about how he found out but also about his dad having diabetes; his dad, he said, had ended up getting really sick and eventually passed away from it. That night it was like Ah'Lee and I shared something that made us bond. After that night, we were official, and nothing or no one could break us up.

3. OUR LIFE

Ah'Lee became the love of my life! Yet, we struggled through a lot of rough times, including arguing and, at times, fighting physically and verbally. Yes, we both played a huge part in the bad times, and we even decided together several times that it would be best if we separated. After separating, though, we always ended up back together because we loved each other.

It seemed like Ah'Lee and I had a "love addiction" for one another. No matter what happened, we couldn't leave each other alone. No matter what he did outside of our home, he respected me, I never allowed anyone to tell me anything negative about him and he did his best to make sure they didn't either. Ah'Lee was like my "go-to" person for everything. No big decisions were made without us discussing them together. Some people wondered why we stayed together after all our struggles, but it was like we didn't care: we were madly in love with each other.

Ah'Lee took care of my kids and he took care of me; we took care of each other, and I was happy. We were happy! Ah'Lee and I hit rough times when he went to jail, and I was left to do everything on my own, but I would make sure I did whatever was necessary to get us back together and keep us above water until he was able to do so himself.

Some people thought Ah'Lee did it all, but he didn't. I had his back, and he knew it because he had mine, and we were loyal to each other, no matter what happened.

Fast forward a few years because if I went into every detail of our relationship, you would be reading forever. What I will say before I move too far ahead is that we ended up finding out that he had an 8-month-old daughter (ZaMaeyah), who was conceived before we were in a relationship. I won't go too far into it, but I love her like she is my own child 'til this day. Ah'Lee and I didn't get to have a child together before he left for reasons I won't speak about, but this little girl was our gift from God. We took care of her like she was our own love child. I have to say "thank you" to her mom for allowing me to be her "other mother"—as some women would have been upset about it.

Now moving ahead a couple of years, Ah'Lee ended up getting really sick. He went to get his blood drawn to have his levels checked; about a month before this visit, his doctor told him he could stop taking his diabetes medicine. After returning from the clinic Ah'Lee looked really pale.

"Are you okay?" I asked, quite concerned.

He said, "Yeah," but explained that he felt bad and almost passed out at the clinic.

"Do you want to lay down?"

"Yeah, for sure," he said.

A friend of mine who was staying with me at the time and had previous experience advised me to take him to the hospital fast—because his blood sugar was either really high or really low! I went to talk to Ah'Lee, and as he began answering my questions, I could smell his breath—it smelled really sweet! He didn't have anything in his mouth, so my friend confirmed: his blood sugar was way too high.

In a bit of a panic, I rushed him to the hospital and, after checking his blood sugar on their hand-held meter, it read high. Waiting for the results of his blood test to return from the lab, I remember Ah'Lee kept falling asleep. Then the doctors came rushing in with bags of insulin and fluids and hooked him up to them.

"What's going on?" I remember asking, and the doctor told me his blood sugar was almost 700—which is a dangerous level—and he could go into a Diabetic coma or shock at any time. Without even thinking, I began praying and asking God to help him. Of course, the doctors ended up admitting him to the hospital, where he stayed for more than a week because they couldn't keep his blood sugar down. They kept trying different kinds of insulin and different amounts—it was crazy! After several attempts they finally got it right, we were able to go home, with Ah'Lee taking two different kinds of insulin four times a day; two different kinds of pills for his diabetes twice a day and check his blood sugar before and after every meal. It was a lot to keep up with and very hard to adjusts to!

That's when I became Ah'Lee's personal nurse and assistant. At least it seemed that way. I kept track of all his medications and when they needed to be refilled, made all doctor appointments, and picked up his medication. It felt like a real full-time job, but I loved him and didn't mind—especially as Ah'Lee took care of me as well, due to my seizures.

So, we both had our fair share of taking care of each other. I would get admitted to the hospital, and Ah'Lee would stay there every night, no matter how late it was. I remember I had to get a test done for 24 hours, with the hospital room lights on the whole time, and while I suspected he wasn't going to want to stay, he actually did. And he never complained. They even gave him the loudest and most uncomfortable bed they could find, but my baby was right by my side.

◆ ◆ ◆

Have you ever had a person you loved or who loved you so much that they were willing to do anything for you? Have you ever had a situation happen in your life and you felt alone, but suddenly God sent something or someone to come and make you feel better? That was what I felt like Ah'Lee was for me: I felt like he was sent from heaven.

SHARE YOUR THOUGHTS..........

4. THEN I MET GOD

Since Ah'Lee and I were doing so well, we ended up moving into a house together in Grandview, Missouri and started working toward taking our relationship to the next level. We talked about getting married, which I took seriously. Marriage was a big deal to me, and I wanted to make sure we were doing it the right way.

Well, it was Easter Sunday, and my cousin told me about her church, Trinity Temple in Grandview, Missouri—which wasn't far from our house. Now, normally I don't go to church on Easter, but this time something told me to go, so I did. Once at the church, I found my cousin and aunt and sat with them. The choir began to sing, and suddenly I felt like I was in a trance. My body started feeling weird, and I started crying. I wanted to stop, but it was like I couldn't stop the tears from falling. The song was amazing, and it made me feel so emotional. I was thinking to myself, *"Girl, why are you crying?"* but I couldn't figure out why. I grabbed some tissue from my aunt and wiped my face because, by this time, I was looking pretty ugly and snot was running down my nose.

I kept thinking to myself, *"What is wrong with me?"* not able to understand. I was crying like I had gotten a whooping or something—it was crazy!

Well, long story short, I ended up staying at that church and going every Sunday. Going every Sunday turned into every Wednesday, which led to my kids attending vacation Bible school as well. I took my children along with me to church, and they loved it. After about four months, I ended up joining the church, which wasn't easy to do. To join, you have to take a series of classes over several weeks to ensure you know not only why you are joining but many important things about the church as well, and, most importantly, about the Father, the Son, and the Holy Spirit.

I learned so much about God, it was like I fell in love with Him—a God addiction, in the best possible way. I remember getting this feeling that was indescribable, and I wanted more of it. It was like I was drunk but not from liquor; I was getting drunk off the Word of God. It was amazing!! I started looking at situations a lot differently, too. For example, I started treating Ah'Lee as if he were my king, my husband, and my other half because in the Bible it says that I was supposed to treat my husband with a patient and respectful love.

I would talk to Ah'Lee about what I was learning, and he seemed to care . . . but he wasn't that interested in going to church himself; we had gone a few times to his mom's church, which I had to talk him into. "I'll just turn around and do the same things, and act the same way when I walk out of the church," he tried to explain to me.

"That doesn't matter," I would counter, "God is a forgiving God, and He already knows what you're going to do. God just wants you to at least try or at least make an effort to change your life. He knows it won't be overnight or easy, but it can be done. Besides, He already knows you and loves you anyway."

So Ah'Lee ended up going to church with me a couple of times, but he wasn't interested. Most of the time, he would say, "I'm good—just call me when you get out."

Now, let me say this before I go any further: Ah'Lee believed in God and prayed before he would touch his food. He prayed every time he felt sick and would pray even harder if I had a seizure. And the reason I know this is because, before I would blackout, he would get a cold rag, put it on my head, and then lean down on the side of the bed and put his head down. When I wake up and regained consciences, he would still be kneeling on the side of the bed. He would then lift his head and say, "Amen!"

I loved that about him: he was a praying man. He did this before I joined the church, so I knew that he knew God. However, I never asked him if he accepted Jesus Christ or know that He died for our sins and rose again on the third day. I didn't ask him that because, at first, I didn't know that was a part of being saved until I started going to the classes. But I have to say that I had a lot of regret at first because, even after I accepted Christ, I didn't ask Ah'Lee if he did as well.

◆ ◆ ◆

Have you ever felt guilty for not asking the proper questions in a situation as serious as this one?

◆ ◆ ◆

However, once I accepted Christ, my life changed!! I discovered what it meant when people said, "I have a personal relationship with God." I used to think people were just talking until I experienced it for myself. I was told in Bible study to talk to God the way you talk to your friends, and at first, I disagreed, *"That can't be right,"* but a lady from church told me that's how you do it. She took me under her wing and taught me all about God's love.

Together, this friend from church and I would read the Word every day and say a prayer before I went to work. So, one day, she asked me to pray, but I told her I didn't know-how. And she said, "I told you to talk to Him like we talk," so that's what I did. And as I was talking to Him, I felt a chill go down my spine and I began to cry. It felt so good—it was crazy—like He came and was sitting right next to me. After that day, I started talking to Him all the time. Jesus became my boy, and God became my daddy. I would talk to Jesus and tell him to translate it to my Daddy for me. It was really cool. I started talking to other people about God and telling them everything I learned about Him. I remember thinking to myself, *"This is pretty cool that I've been talking to Him like this."*

Tanika K. Judie

I learned so much about God that I didn't know; I even went to a book store and got a book that was called *The Story*, which is the Bible in the form of a novel. It impacted me so much—all the stuff I was reading—like I was reading a fiction book, except it was true. God was kind of like a gangster; He didn't play no games. If you didn't do what He said, He would turn you into salt. He even burned down cities if you were sinning. God was the Truth then and still is. I like that about Him because He reminded me of me, just in a good way.

Have you accepted Jesus Christ as your Lord and Savior? Do you know what it means to be saved? If you haven't accepted Christ, it's not too late to do so, and if you don't know what it means to be saved, don't worry because below I'll tell you again.

However, before I do, I want you to know that once you accept Christ, your life will change. but perhaps not immediately, and it won't be easy—trust me, I know. But, He will forgive you and will never leave your side. All He requires is that

you have faith as small as a mustard seed and trust Him with your life because He will never forsake you.

Believe in the Lord Jesus, and you will be saved. – Acts 16:31 (NTL)

*God has already done all the work. All you
must do is receive, in faith, the salvation God*

offers. – Ephesians 2:8-9 (NTL)

Fully trust in Jesus alone as the payment for your sins. Believe in Him, and you will not perish. – John 3:16 (NTL)

God is offering you salvation as a gift. All you must do is accept it. Jesus is the way of salvation. – John 14:6 (NTL)

Tell the Lord that you realize you're a sinner. Tell God you repent of your sins and have changed your mind about going your old ways. Say, **"Father in Heaven, I believe that Jesus died for my sins."** And God will impart eternal life to your spirit.

Share Your thoughts..........

5. ONE STEP FORWARD, TWO STEPS BACK

After doing well for about six to seven months, something happened, and I stopped going to church as much. Once I fell away from attending church every Sunday, I somehow allowed some negative or harmful actions and attitudes to resurface—and I started doing them again. I knew this wasn't what God wanted for me.

I wasn't drinking as much, but I was hanging out a lot and just doing things that I know weren't pleasing to God. Ah'Lee was still doing his usual, and even asking me on Sundays if I was going to church. And I would get mad and ask, "Why, are you?"

He would look at me with attitude and shock, "Are you serious?"

And I would say, "Exactly," and roll back over.

He eventually stopped asking. I had kind of given up on living the right way. *"It takes too much effort to do the right thing"* is what I told myself. The excuses were so good that I let them consume my mind, and I even started questioning what I thought I felt before. I wondered if it were even real.

I'm sure you're wondering why I did this, why I let it happen. Well, I wish I could tell you why. My thoughts started spiraling to areas that weren't good for me, and I didn't try to fight it. I basically just let it happen because it felt good. Then tragedy struck, and I was left really feeling like God was mean and didn't really save people like I thought he did.

On September 12, 2015, a good friend of mine, someone I called my brother, was killed. After he left this earth, it was like I got mad at God and wanted an explanation as to why He took him from his children and all the people who loved him. Death wasn't new to me at all, but it still hurt. I was so tired of people dying in my life—and it was crazy how many were dying.

From 2006 through 2010, it seemed like I lost somebody I loved every year.

Let me back up to the very first loss. I had a boyfriend who was killed on 71 Highway on his way to my house in 2006, but on top of that, I had lost our baby as well. At this time, I prayed, but God wasn't my Friend like He wanted to be, or I'll say I didn't have a personal relationship with Him—I only knew of Him.

Then in February 2007, I lost the father of my two oldest children. He was shot in a drive-by shooting while putting gas in his friend's car. That left me alone with my two oldest kids. When he passed, I was dating someone else and I was pregnant. Not only was I pregnant, but I was pregnant with twins. I remember my twins' father telling me that he would help me, and I didn't have to worry about anything.

Well, why did he say that? Because March 31, 2007, just five weeks after I lost my first kids' father, my twins' father was also killed in a drive-by shooting. Now, I was left alone to take care of two children as well as the two on the way.

I felt like it was all my fault like I was bad luck like I just couldn't get a break. I was very emotional and just depressed. I didn't want to eat or anything—it was horrible. I was starving the babies I was carrying, and to top it off, I was having more seizures that would cut off their oxygen—every time I had one.

So, I had to turn into the Tin Man and try to be heartless. Keep in mind, when I was a little girl, I hated that movie, *The Wizard of Oz*, because the Tin Man used to scare me, but then I found myself becoming him.

The very next year, 2008, I ended up losing my very good friend, named Braids; he was the one person who made sure that my kids and I were okay, but then he was gone. After that, I blacked out for about a year. Yes, it's true. Most of my memories of that time are gone, just like they died, too. Crazy how your mind has a way of shielding yourself from the pain.

In 2010, I lost another friend whom I had just been with minutes before he died. I was actually on my way to meet back up with him when I pulled up to a car accident—it was him in the car and I had to basically identify him to the officers on the scene! Is that enough to make one person go insane?

❖ ❖ ❖

How do you keep faith in God after all the things He's put you through? Why trust Him after that, right? I'm sure you're wondering why you should, but please keep reading, and I'll tell you.

Share Your thoughts..........

6. WHY?

I was so mad at God, I didn't know what to do. He kept stealing the people I loved, and He still wasn't helping me understand why. So of course, my anger turned more inward, and I started resenting Him. I would pray, but nothing else. Going to church was not an option for me unless someone invited me, and even then, I barely wanted to go. I had carried on with my life, not even feeling bad for sinning at times, just doing stuff and not caring—because I felt like He didn't care about me.

When he took my brother, it took me over the edge, so I thought, "*Oh, well.*" Yet I still prayed often and asked God "*why?*" But he never answered me.

This went on for months, but then somehow, He drew me back into attending church—and from my viewpoint, I thought it would help me out. Well, it did help me, but it didn't give me answers as to why all these people that I loved had died.

I was still mad, but I ended up becoming scared of God in away. I started thinking about all the things He did to people in the Bible and what He did to my loved ones, which had me questioning myself. "*Who am I?*" So, I prayed and asked God to forgive me, but kept doing the same stuff.

It was like I did just enough for Him to forgive me, but not enough to where He would think that I wasn't mad at Him anymore. I even started telling people about God again, even I didn't believe some of the things I was telling them: I was a sad case. It was like the stuff I was telling people would just come out. I didn't know where it came from, but it was good stuff! So, I started writing some of my prayers down and journaling like I used to do when I was a kid. I would go back and read my prayers to see if it would help, *but still nothing.* Now, don't get me wrong: I was still mad, all at the same time, but I didn't want Him to punish me. I know that sounds bad, but it's the truth.

I was so mad at Him I didn't know what to do!! I was tired of Him taking people without warning, without saying why, and without at least helping me heal from it. I would just bury the pain and say, *"I'll deal with it another time."* As I kept burying stuff, the fuller my backyard got, but I still didn't—or I'll say couldn't—accept it. I left all those people there so I could go back to them one day; I couldn't let them go because I had no closure. I was hanging on to all those souls because I wasn't ready for them to leave, and God didn't give me any explanation. I would write them letters, hoping they would talk to me in some way, but nothing happened. I had dreams about them and knew they were okay, but my dreams didn't tell me what I needed to hear, and so that wasn't good enough. So, back to the backyard, they went.

I know everyone has experienced bad things happening in their lives, but I didn't understand why they were happening to me—feeling like my faith in God should have been like a protective shield from anything bad or sad. I still don't fully understand why all the tragedy came my way, but now I look at it all differently. *"This is way too much for one person to endure,"* or so I thought, but little did I know things would get worse.

◆ ◆ ◆

Have you ever felt like you were mad at God because you wanted to know something or prayed for something, and He wouldn't answer you or send you a sign or nothing? Have you ever been so mad that you wanted to throw the whole Bible away? Have you ever just asked God "why?"—asked God why He allowed something to take place in your life, but never got your answer?

Well, I have on more than one occasion, but then He did something that had me talking to Him like I was when I had my first encounter with Him.

❖ ❖ ❖

Share Your thoughts..........

7. I SAID "YES!"

May 24, 2016

Jumping forward again, I pray you keep up and I don't lose you —because my life has been all over the place. It was a sunny day, and I was fresh off work and on my way home when Ah'Lee called me. He told me to meet him on 47th Street. I said okay because it was normal for Ah'Lee to meet me, either at home or somewhere between home and my job downtown (which he visited often, bringing me lunch), or we would just sit on face-time for hours. Anyway, I pulled up, and he came and got in the car with me.

Ah'Lee was smiling from ear to ear. We embraced each other, and Ah'Lee was smiling like he saw something funny or he was happy about something. I remember saying, "What's up? You must have missed me."

He replied with his normal response, "I always do." Then he pulled out this black box, then I was smiling from ear to ear, too. Ali had taken me to a store and gotten my ring size months ago, but to actually see this box took me to another place.

I was like, "What are you about to do, Buddy?" (Buddy was my nickname for him.)

"Let me see your hand," he said.

"Which one?" I smiled back.

"Stop playing," he grinned with that beautiful smile that always captured my heart. I gave him my left hand and smiled so hard that my face started hurting. Ah'Lee opened the box, and I couldn't believe how beautiful the ring was. It was perfect: big, with white gold and a lot of diamonds.

I looked up at him and started laughing, saying, "Are you serious?"

"Do you like it?" he asked.

"Yes, I sure do."

He took the ring out the box and started talking.

"Wait," I said. I pulled out my phone and pressed record. And Ah'Lee kept right on talking. He seemed so nervous while he was talking . . . it was so cute.

"You know I love you, right?" he asked.

"Yes," I answered.

"You know I want to be with you forever, right?" he asked. "I want to get married, build our family, and everything."

I said, "Okay, so what are you saying?" eager for him to get to the point.

"So this is a promise that we're going to make it happen." He looked at me with so much love in his eyes.

"Make what happen, Buddy?" I said with a twinkle in my eyes, too.

"Marriage, babies, all that," he replied.

"Are you proposing?"

"I am."

"Okay, yes!" I gushed.

He put the ring on my finger and said, "Now can you fit it?" I pushed it down into its new place on my finger, and said, "Yes," and kissed him.

Oh, how I loved that man. He was my everything.

I asked him why he loved me, and he said, "Because you have a good heart and for a lot of other reasons."

"Okay, well, do you fall in love with me all over again every day?" (I asked him that because I heard a lady ask her husband that in a movie.)

"Yes."

I said, "No, I'm serious, do you? "

"Yeah, because you make me happy, your heart is good, you're a good person, and for a lot of other reasons, Tamika."

I said, "Okay," again and looked him in the eyes and kissed him once more.

I knew he was being truthful because of the way he looked at me. The look in his eyes told me everything I needed to know.

Ah'Lee was my other half, and I knew he would be from

the day I first saw him in the "after-hours." I was so in love with him. The look in his eyes was so pure and deep, I couldn't do anything but love on him. His eyes told me everything all the time. If he wasn't being truthful, if he was sad, if he didn't feel good, if he was mad, stressed—anything he was feeling—I could see it through those pretty, chestnut eyes.

A few days later we made plans to have our wedding on Oct. 7, 2017. The date was chosen because it was the birthday of my grandmother who had passed away. Plus, 7 is my favorite number, and 10+7=17. It was perfect. I knew that 7 is also the number of completion, and once we wedded, we would be whole.

At first, Ah'Lee didn't want to have a big wedding. We were thinking we could go off and get married or go to the courthouse and then come and have a big reception. I agreed because I feel like people spend a lot of money on big weddings for other people, and you get too stressed out trying to get it together. But then I was like, *"Well, I've always dreamed of this day, so I want everyone to see how happy we are and how much we love each other."*

"It's whatever you want to do," Ah'Lee said. I told him I wanted a wedding, but it didn't matter where it was or if we didn't have an actual wedding; just as long as we were getting married, I didn't care. As long as I was marrying this man, we could have gotten married on a Sunday after church service or in a parking lot. The wedding didn't matter that much, for real; it was the fact that he chose me to be his wife that got me. To have someone love you that much and you feel the same is amazing. We were head-over-heels in love with each other. Some people may not agree, but I don't care, because I knew another side of Ah'Lee that nobody else did. He took care of me, and not just financially, but in a way that no other man has ever done. The way he made me feel was crazy.

I've always been one to give myself to a person without thinking twice about it, but this time was different. Ah'Lee and I knew we would grow old together, no matter what came our way. We had our issues, but none of that could out-weigh our love. The crazy thing is, I don't think either one of us knew that we could love someone other than our children in this way. It was like a drug. We were so in sync with each other: I would think about him and look at my phone, and he would text me or call me, and vice versa. We would respond or answer and say, "I was just thinking about you when you texted (or called)." We would laugh, and I would say, "Get outta my head, Buddy."

Note: I called Ah'Lee "Buddy" because of the toy back in the day called "My Buddy." It had a song that went with it and all. The song says: "My buddy. My buddy. Everywhere I go, he goes. My buddy. Everywhere I go, he goes. My buddy and me like to climb up a tree, my buddy and I are the best friends that could be! My buddy (My buddy) My buddy and me!" That's exactly how I felt about him, except we weren't climbing trees—we were climbing huge obstacles in our life and relationship.

Anyway, let me get back to the wedding because I could go on and on about the love we shared. Ah'Lee and I were watching TV, and Remy Ma was getting married; Ah'Lee was super tuned in to the show. He was looking super serious, so at the end of the show, I asked him, "You like that?"

"Yeah," he answered, looking at me. It was kinda crazy 'cause there was like a fire in his eye.

I asked, "You want to have a big wedding, baby?"

"Yeah, I do," he replied.

After that, I was even more excited and started making plans. I started going to different venues, checking prices, and looking for dresses. This was really happening. *"I'm going to marry the love of my life!"* I thought, not even realizing that this man, my Buddy, would not make it to our big day.

◆ ◆ ◆

Have you ever wanted something so bad that you made plans toward it every day, then when that time comes, it doesn't happen? How did that make you feel? It doesn't have to be a wedding—it can be anything. To anticipate something so dear to you and then have it taken away can deeply damage a person. It was things and thoughts like this that made me question my entire existence.

Share Your thoughts...........

8. SAVED

September 13, 2016

It was three days after my birthday, and I had taken a trip to St. Louis with Ah'Lee, my cousins, and my sister and brother. We left on September 10 (which is my birthday) and came back the next day, the 11th.

Yet the day before leaving, we partied hard at this club called Rookies on 85th Street, then drove to Westport and stayed there until almost daylight. Finally, at home, we got about an hour of sleep, and then got up early and were right back at it. After buying more liquor, we hit the road for St. Louis— where we partied all night once again. The St. Louis clubs close at 6 a.m., so we didn't close our eyes to sleep until around 7. Since we were all wasted, we didn't end up leaving until around 1 p.m. that next day. On the long drive back, Ah'Lee and I had a good time in the car, singing and rapping to our favorite songs. Ah'Lee was a totally different person around me than with other people, and I loved to see him so open. Some people wouldn't believe the type of person he really was with me and our children.

But getting back to the story, I figured all this would be cool because I had September 12th off and I would rest that day. Well, that didn't happen as I planned. I ended up doing everything else but rest, and the next day I paid for it.

> **Note:** *Keep in mind, I have Epilepsy, and one of the triggers is lack of sleep. My doctors had also told me that excessive drinking lowers the seizure threshold—meaning the chances to have one go down. But the minute the alcohol wears off, the seizure threshold goes way up, making me at higher risk for a seizure. Of course, I wasn't thinking*

about any of that while I was partying for my birthday.

I woke up on September 13th feeling horrible. I just knew that I was going to be sick, but I tried to catch it before it came by taking my medicine, putting a cold towel on my head, and going back to sleep. At the time I was working at Research Medical Center as a registrar, and I didn't have to be at work until 3 p.m., so I had enough time to lay back down and go to sleep. After sleeping for about 4 hours, I figured I would be refreshed, but not so much. I actually woke up feeling worse.

I felt like my body was shutting down—my head was hurting bad like someone had hit me in the head with a bat. I felt weak and just all the way off. I walked into the front room where Ah'Lee was sitting and told him I still felt terrible.

"Aw, babe, do you think you can make it into work?" he asked.

"Well, I have to because I've already been off for three days," I lamented.

"Are you sure, baby, because you don't look so good," he asked, the concern pouring from his eyes.

"Yeah, I'm cool," I assured him, not really believing it myself. I was going to take some more medicine and lay back down.

"Okay, but if you don't feel better, you really shouldn't go," he advised. Of course, anyone who knows me knows that I'm super hard-headed, and when it comes to my money, I will go to work; I don't care how I'm feeling. So, after taking more medicine, I laid back down until it was time to get ready.

Surprisingly, I did get up and got myself together for work, kissed Buddy, and told him I was leaving.

"Call me when you make it there," he said, still not believing I was walking out the door.

"Sure, okay," I remember saying, and left the house. But as you might expect, I remember driving to work and feeling like I was about to blackout. I started praying and asking God to help me make it to work safely—just like a typical person praying and talking to God when they need something, huh? However, at the time that was me.

So, God answered my prayer, and I made it to work safely.

NOTE: Be careful what you ask God for because he gave me just that and nothing more. I should have asked him to help me period.

I parked my car and remember walking into the emergency department, where I was working that night, but my vision started getting blurry. I sat down and took a few deep breaths, then called to the person checking the patients in, asking if she could check me in as well!

She laughed and said, tongue-in-cheek, "Sure, Tamika, anything for you."

She thought I was playing because we joked around a lot to make time go faster. Yet, this time I was serious, but she kept doing her work and playing me off. So, I got up to walk over to her, but by that time she was already checking in another patient. I remember looking around for a nurse because I knew I was about to blackout—I could feel it—but I couldn't see a nurse anywhere. I walked out into the hallway and spotted my favorite nurse. "*Thank God!!*" I remember thinking.

I reached out to her and she asked, "Are you okay?"

I looked at her, barely able to speak, but managed to mumble, "No . . ."

"Honey, you don't look good," she said, looking into my eyes.

The next thing I remember, I was lying on the table, wondering what happened, trying to figure out where I was, and wondering why the heck my shirt was off. I remember the doctors asking all kinds of questions that I couldn't answer. They asked about my phone and for my code as well. However, I couldn't remember it. They checked my file and found my mother's number, I think, and called her. The events after that were a blur. I was in and out. I later found out that I had multiple seizures back to back that day, which resulted in me being admitted in the hospital for two long weeks.

During my hospital stay, I remember talking to God, asking Him why I was there, why He was allowing me to keep having seizures, why He had me in this situation, period. I went through a lot while in the hospital. The doctor treating me ended up overdosing me—and then treating me for symptoms I was having due to the overdose of medications. I started having problems with my blood pressure dropping low when I stood up. I found that if I didn't eat, I would get light-headed, dizzy, and blackout. I had to have all kinds of tests on my heart as well for my blood pressure. The doctor treating me was making all kinds of stuff go wrong in my body.

I was really scared, I can't lie. I didn't know what was going to happen. I couldn't remember anything during my first week in the hospital because of the number of seizures wracking my body and brain. Then finally, four days before I was released, a new doctor came in per request from my family and checked my chart; he started doing some tests to see what was going on. He was the one who told me that I had been given way too much medication, and everything going on was side effects to that. Talk about frustrating! He broke it down for us while trying not to throw his colleague under the bus. I was angry but also grateful that he figured it out because I was ready to go home.

Believe it or not, while I was in the hospital, I often found myself praying and waiting on God to answer me. I knew that He was having me go through this for a reason, and I was determined to figure out why. I prayed every day and even would turn on worship music, listening to every word in detail, trying to find a sign, phrase, or word that stuck out that would reveal what God wanted me to get from all this.

While in the hospital, I reflected on a time I was in the hospital previously, having seizures back to back without knowing where they were coming from. I remember I felt like I was dreaming one time while having a seizure. Everything was black, and I felt like I was trying to pull myself up out of a hole or out of the darkness. I remember seeing a small light-up high and trying to get to it, then after multiple attempts, I gave up and ended up waking up in the hospital bed. I felt like I was dead at that time, and this time I felt the same, or like I was going to die. The only difference this time was that I felt like I was going to die in real life, not just in a dream. I felt like the seizures were going to kill me. Then it hit me: I must get my life right with God —that's what this was all about. I must stop being mad about things I can't change because God is God, and He can take me out at any time. It may sound crazy, but after days of trying to figure it out, that's what I felt God was impressing on my heart.

Before I left the hospital, I made up my mind that I would start walking the right way. I told myself that I was going to talk to Ah'Lee and ask him if he would like to go on this walk with me, and if he didn't, then forget all of this—I'm out. Yes, out of my relationship with him. We wouldn't be getting married or anything—that's how deeply I felt this new conviction. *"I'm willing to walk away from it all to go to heaven,"* I decided.

I was so nervous about talking to Ah'Lee; I wanted him to walk with me so we could both get closer to God, but if he didn't, I was going to have to make the hardest move I'd ever made—and that was leaving him. I told myself I would ask him if he wanted to walk this journey with God and give him a chance to say "yes" or "no"—without telling him that if he didn't, then I was leaving. You see, I didn't want to force him to do it so we could be together—because then it wouldn't be genuine. I feel like this is what God wanted because I ended up leaving the hospital two days later. Although I was happy to get out, I was sad and nervous about what I thought I may have to do.

❖ ❖ ❖

Have you ever been in a situation that you didn't know if you would make it out alive or not? Did you call out to God and wait for Him to come to you in some way or another? Have you ever had to make a decision that was good for you but may hurt someone else? Life is crazy like that. We get hit with all kinds of different things. We feel like we have it all figured out, but then we get hit with a wild card and end up feeling like we may lose if we don't think fast.

Share Your thoughts..........

9. HERE GOES NOTHING

October 3, 2016

I was free from the hospital, thank God, and on my way home. I couldn't wait to get home to my bed and my kids—I missed them so much. I remember my daughter called me when I was in the hospital and sung me one of my favorite songs by Tasha Cobbs ("For Your Glory"). She had me in tears, but also made me fight harder to get home to her and my other kids. So, I was super excited to see them. Ah'Lee was there waiting also, and I couldn't wait to lay under him. They were my safety and sanity!

While on the ride home, I remember thinking about Ah'Lee and how I was going to talk to him about walking this new journey with me. I was so nervous! But it had to be done. I remember praying and asking God to help me—and I prayed that Ah'Lee would have an open heart to receive it. Once at home, I laid down to wait for my children to arrive from school and to rest because I was getting short of breath. My mom had picked me up from the hospital and was going to stay the night to help us out. That was perfect because I wasn't going to make it moving around too much; I felt like an old lady! I slept for a little while, and finally, it was time for my babies to get home. I hid in my room until they arrived—momma told them to bring her something from the hallway, and that's when I walked out. They were so happy! We were all in tears. I love my kiddos so much!! They are my everything, and I have to say they let me know I am theirs!! Ah'Lee came home and, of course, I was happy, and so was he. He was kinda in and out because my momma was there to help me, so it gave me more time to get my words and thoughts together. I had no idea how I was going to pull this off, but I prayed that it would work.

October 4, 2016

The next day, Ah'Lee took me to the doctor for my follow-up visit. I remember her being very upset about what the first doctor did to me in the hospital. Ah'Lee and I both expressed how we felt about it, too. After we left, we decided to go get some food at Steak and Shake in Raymore, Missouri (one of our favorite places because we ate a lot for under $20). On the ride there, I remember not saying too much, just kinda riding and holding his hand, which was our normal thing. I was thinking the whole ride, like, *"Can I do this? Will I have the guts to let go if he doesn't want this? How am I going to say this without making him feel pressured?"* I had all these thoughts running through my head. I said a silent prayer and said, *"I got this, I think."*

We pulled up to Steak and Shake, and as we were walking in, I was thinking, *"When should I say it? When? When?"* I was all over the place.

Moving forward, we ordered our food, finished eating, and ended up getting some shakes. While drinking up that yummy, cold treat, I decided it was time.

I began hesitantly, "Ah'Lee, I think we really need to talk."

"Okay, about what?"

"Oh, nothing bad, just something I been thinking about."

"Yeah, okay, what's up?"

"Ah'Lee, while I was in the hospital I was thinking and trying to figure out why God was allowing me to go through all that," I let the words spill out. "I was praying and waiting on God to tell me something. I waited and waited—and the only thing that I came up with was I need to start walking with God. I need to get my life back together because, honestly, I was scared, and I want to go to heaven."

Ah'Lee sat there quiet, just listening like he normally did.

"So, I want to know if you will take this walk with me?" I held my breath and waited on him to respond.

Ah'Lee looked at me and without hesitation, he said, "Yeah, I will!"

I remember saying, "Huh, you will?!"

He said matter-of-factly, "Yeah, what do I have to do—or what do we do?"

I was so happy!! My ears kinda went up, I was smiling, and I wanted to hug him and kiss him, but I had to keep my cool because he didn't know what I was going to have to do if he had said "no." Then I thought to myself, *"This man is amazing. He wants to love God on his own, not because I'm making him do it. This is real! I didn't have to pressure him or anything. God, You sent me an angel!!"*

I got out of my head and told him, "Well, first you have to accept Christ as your Lord and Savior . . . Do you accept Him?"

And he said, "Yes, I do."

I asked him, "Do you believe that Jesus died on the cross for your sins and rose again?"

He said, "Yes!"

I said, "Okay, well, next we can start reading the Bible and praying together so we can get closer to God and learn His Word. We both have to develop a personal relationship with Him."

Ah'Lee said, "Okay!"

"So we can start reading tonight, but before we read, we will pray and ask God for an understanding of what we are about to read. Then we can talk about it so we can make sure we both get it. Okay?" I smiled, astonished by all that God was doing in both of our lives.

Ah'Lee said, "Okay, I'm ready."

I was so shocked by what had just happened that I didn't say anything else. I just let it sink in and finished my shake. I was so in love with him and couldn't wait for us to fall in love with God together.

❖ ❖ ❖

Ask yourself, *"Are you willing to do whatever it takes to be saved? Are you willing to do whatever it takes to get to heaven or at least try to get to heaven?"* Those are questions that I never asked myself, but I ended up making a decision based on the events that took place in my life. I challenge you to share your journey or walk with God with someone else. I challenge you to ask someone, *"Can you walk with me on this journey because I don't know how to do it on my own?"* You'll be surprised how many people really want to be saved and try but don't know how, or how many people would love to share their walk with you because it can be lonely.

Speak up, and you can save someone's life or someone can save yours. God used me to do it, and Buddy got saved. As hard as it was to approach him, to speak those words, he said, "Yes!" I challenge you to try it for yourself.

Tanika K. Judie

Share Your thoughts..........

10. THE JOURNEY

Ah'Lee and I started our new journey soon after we left that day. I remember going to church that Sunday and talking to this lady whom I often spoke to, and I told her about the decision we made. I asked her where we should start reading in the Bible, and she said, "Galatians would be a great place!" She told me to start there because it talks about being free from bondage and we have to get away from the worldly things—habits and attitudes that were not pleasing to God.

"Thank you so much!" I said and went home to share all this with Ah'Lee. He was still at home, thank God, because most of the time he would be gone around 2:00 p.m., which is when I got out of church. I relayed, word for word, all that the lady at church told me.

"Okay!" he said.

And I followed with, "Then let's start tonight." Ah'Lee agreed, which was such a shock to me as I thought he would have changed his mind by now. Yet, he hadn't! I was happy because that meant he wanted it for himself. I was super excited and even decided to do a Bible study with my children at home on Thursdays, so they can learn more about God with me and Ah'Lee. We were all headed in the right direction, and for the first time and a long time, I felt like we would be cool.

Later that night, Ah'Lee came home and I asked him, "So, are you ready to read?"

Ah'Lee said, "yea," and sat down on the bed.

I said to myself, *"Here goes nothing."* I turned my Bible to Galatians and then set it down. I grabbed Ah'Lee's hand and told him we had to pray before we read.

He said, "Okay," and I began to pray.

"God, we come to you today asking that you touch me and

Ah'Lee's mind and heart so that we may receive the Word and apply it to our lives. I ask that you help us understand it and hear what we need to hear as we read. I ask this in the name of your Son, Jesus, Amen!"

After we prayed, I began to read. We read one full chapter, and then I stopped and looked up at Ah'Lee. He was sitting there quiet.

"Ah'Lee?"

"Yes."

"Let's just read one chapter at a time so we won't get over-whelmed."

"Sounds good."

"Do you understand what I just read?" I asked.

He answered, "Yeah, I think so."

I remember saying, "Good," and I told him what I thought it meant.

"I feel the same way," he said.

I gave Ah'Lee an example of how it can apply to our lives. Ah'Lee agreed, and we finished our night. I was happy knowing he was really listening, and it felt good to have him really being a part of it. I then reminded Ah'Lee that we still have to pray together when he was home and when he was out. He agreed.

"When you're not home, then we can facetime one another so we can pray," I suggested.

Ah'Lee even agreed to that! I didn't think he was really going to facetime me and pray in front of his people, but he proved me wrong.

One night, Ah'Lee had left after we read for that day, but later, I wanted to pray with him before going to sleep, so I face timed him. Ah'Lee was surrounded by dudes laughing, talking loud, and having a good time. I just knew that he was about to shoot me down, so I got an attitude before he could even respond—but I didn't say anything; I just patiently waited to go off after he told me "no." To my surprise, Ah'Lee said, "Okay, let me go outside real quick." I remember being super shocked and switching my attitude real quick as well.

I said, "Okay," trying not to sound super excited.

When Ah'Lee got outside, he said, "Ok, come on."

I said, "You pray this time."

He said, "I don't know how to pray, so you gotta do it." I told Ah'Lee what my friend from church told me about praying and how it was just talking to God like you're having a conversation with a friend.

Ah'Lee said, "That's cool, but you pray."

I laughed and went ahead and prayed. We said, "Amen," and I said, "I love you, Ah'Lee, and I'll see you when you get home." That was just the first night of our many facetime prayers. I was so happy about our journey and happy about how it was changing our relationship.

Ah'Lee used to be very secretive; or let me rephrase that, he was very protective about his past, emotions, and feelings. He would be stressed about something and would keep it to himself, or I would have to beg him to tell me so I could help him. Ah'Lee told me bits and pieces of his past and childhood but not too much. I used to ask him why he wouldn't talk about it, and he said it wasn't anything to talk about. However, I would catch him in deep thought with his eyes blood-shot red. I would even catch Ah'Lee crying from time to time. He shared some stuff that was bothering him, but he never wanted to make people look bad or for him to look weak, so he wouldn't go too far.

Ah'Lee told me what he felt I needed to know, but he felt like the stuff that stressed him the most was his problem. He would say, "I want to be able to take care of things," but when he couldn't, it was hard on him. One day when Ah'Lee was crying, he said it was because he was thinking about his dad and really missed him. Ah'Lee was going through some deep stuff but refused to let it out. I would pray and ask God to continue to guide us and to allow Ah'Lee to open up more. He was starting to open up and tell me sometimes why he was stressed or frustrated, but other times he still wouldn't. We continued to read and pray every day, and we started talking more, not only about our past situations but also present things that bothered us, even about our families and the situations we were going through with them. We decided that we would help each other out with anything we could and just go from there. This made our relationship so much stronger.

I knew it was all God because it all started to come together after we started praying and reading. Now, don't think it was easy and we didn't still have problems, because that would be a lie. We still had a lot of work to do, but we were going in the right direction. Relationships between the two of us and between us and our children were growing and thriving.

About this time, Ah'Lee also started to have some health issues that scared me. He started losing a lot of weight, dropping from a 38-inch waist to a 34 in two months. He started to have some issues affecting certain organs in his body. and I knew something was wrong. I first thought it was stress, but then something told me to call the doctor because this was serious — and getting worse. I made an appointment, and I'm glad I did because Ah'Lee's A1C had gone off the chart. It was over 14, a number so high that the doctor's monitor couldn't even record the exact number. Ah'Lee ended up having to take more insulin and pills to bring it down. He hated taking shots but knew that if he wanted to live, he would have to swallow them like a man. Although he was really discouraged and upset about it, we kept praying and following the doctor's orders.

Slowly, Ah'Lee started gaining some weight back and was doing a little better. But it seemed that just when he started opening up to me and we were doing better, the enemy hit us by attacking his health. It sucked, but I just knew that God would heal him or at least make it better.

◆ ◆ ◆

Have you ever tried hard to get close to God, but it seemed like you got hit with something that could have taken your life or someone you loved? Even if it wasn't that serious, have you had the enemy come in and throw distraction after distraction at you to steal your focus? Well, sad to say, that's what his job is: to kill, steal, and destroy—but he can only do that if you allow it. I know it's easier said than done, but trust me, if you keep pushing and praying, you will get through whatever he throws your way.

Share Your thoughts..........

11. SUCH A GENTLEMAN

February 14, 2017

Valentine's Day is my favorite holiday for women. Well, Mother's Day is, too, but Valentine's Day was better for me because I got to see Ah'Lee in a more open and vulnerable way. Ah'Lee would always get me something and take me out to eat, so while I was looking forward to it, this Valentine's Day was different. I remember him waking me up by kissing me and saying, "Happy Valentine's Day!" I got up to get ready for work, wanting to look extra pretty because I knew Ah'Lee and I was going to celebrate in a special way: I had asked Ah'Lee to make it personal and nothing simple.

Ah'Lee told me that it would be special because he had something in mind. I said, "Okay, we shall see." Ah'Lee wasn't very romantic and didn't know how to come up with unique stuff as I did. Well, except when we went out of town for his birthday the year before. He was a totally different person when we were out of town, and we had such a good time! We didn't want to leave. Getting back to Valentine's Day, all was proceeding like normal. We facetime for most of the day, which was our everyday thing. And I remember thinking, *"He doesn't have anything planned because he's been on the phone with me all day."*

I got off work, called Ah'Lee to see where he was, and he said, "At home."

I said, "Okay, I'm on my way." I pulled up, went into the house, put my stuff up, and went into the kitchen to see the kids, and my mouth dropped. There was a humongous balloon on the table, a dozen roses, a chocolate heart, and a big basket with candy and my favorite Victoria secret perfume and panties in it. All I could do was smile. The kids were standing there smiling, as one of them hit the balloon and it started singing, "I got my mind stayed on you!" I started laughing and asked, "Where's

Ah'Lee?"

They said, "In the bedroom, Momma."

I went back there, and he was lying in bed, smiling from ear to ear. I said, "Thank you, Buddy, I love it."

"You're welcome," he answered, giving me a kiss.

I said, "You know, that balloon was singing to me, right? So now, you gotta sing the same words, what it says to me."

He laughed and said, "I can't sing!"

I said, "So sing it anyway." I hit the balloon, it started singing, and Ah'Lee sang along with it. I laughed but was super happy.

After that I got the kids settled and Ah'Lee said he wanted to take me to Top Golf to eat and play golf. I told him "That's cool." And the whole night there, Ah'Lee made me feel like a queen. He did everything right; he was very gentle with me and just super sweet. I was so happy and felt like I was falling in love with him for the first time and for the millionth time. That was my Buddy, and I loved him so much. I kept telling him all night that he had made my day. He made me so happy, not because of what he gave me but because he opened up and did something new. God was really working on him, I could tell. I wanted more days and dates like this, but sadly, this would be the last holiday we shared together.

◆ ◆ ◆

Ever feel like you were dreaming when something good happened in your life, and you never wanted to wake up because it was just that good? That's how I felt that Valentine's Day—during our amazing, "mind stayed on you," perfect day together.

STOP . . . .

Before I start the next chapter, I have to say it was the hardest chapter to write. I prayed about it and asked God to guide my hands and allow me to tell my story the way He wants me to. I asked Him to allow me to be transparent, so people will know where I was in my mind and in my heart. I told God I want others to know the reality of it all, so I asked Him to help me be selfless and take my emotions out of it until I finish writing.

However, all that didn't seem to help much. My mind said, "*Write*," but my heart said, "*No, don't go back to that place.*"

I started having all kinds of anxiety about it, and I stopped writing for a little while because I knew that this chapter would bring those feelings and emotions back to life. My reality would hit me in the face, and just at the time that I was starting to allow my Buddy to be free. Not only was I getting to where I could release him, but my children's fathers as well—all the people and things I've lost in life. I wasn't ready, but God had other plans.

God told me that He has me. He wants me to tell it all and not hold anything back. God told me that my story will help millions of people if I tell it. I remember going back and forth with God-like, "*No, I can't do it.*"

But He responded with, "Yes, you can, and you will. This is only the beginning of what I will have you do."

He told me, "You didn't know you were going to write this book, but I put it on your lap. I set it all up for you. I had you

Tanika K. Judie

go see a movie about me, so I could show you what I needed you to do. When you started writing, you didn't know it would flow so easy, but it did. You trust Me, don't you?" He asked.

I said, "Yes."

And He said, "So trust me now."

I looked up at the ceiling in my room and said, "Ugh . . ."

Then God continued to speak, saying, "I do everything for a reason, and this has nothing to do with you personally, but everything to do with Me.

"As you do all I show you, more people will know something so important: even as they go through things that seem unfair, I will turn it all around for their good if they trust Me."

"You see, Tamika," I heard Him say, "there's always a purpose for what you go through and deal with on earth, but the problem is that people lose sight of the greatest thing—ME!!! I am the highest, and if you continue to focus on Me in the midst of the storm, I will direct your path and show you the sun. I know it's hard; it's hard for me, too."

He continued, "I allowed my Son to come to earth and show you the way. I then allowed my Son to experience all the pain and slander He received—for you. After all, He went through, I then let my Son die on a cross in pain for your sins—and for the sins of people who still won't trust Me. Some people question Me and ask why, but it was all for you to be able to get what I promised you in the beginning: Eternal Life."

I was like, "Okay, God, okay, I get it now, and You can stop!!"

So, after all that, here goes nothing! —just the raw and uncut, all the way through. I hope God is pleased.

12. IM STILL GOING

Early March 2017

Ah'Lee and I had made plans to go to Texas for the weekend to see his sister. I booked and paid for the room and got everything set up. It was his birthday month, and we planned to be out of town every weekend that month, going to places we hadn't been before. I was super excited, and he was, too. In the days leading up to us leaving, I was getting everything ready and even bought us both some new stuff to take with us.

Well, at the last minute, Ah'Lee decided he didn't want to go to Texas because he wanted to save some money for the other weekend trips and make some more money by staying home as well.

I was so mad at him, I wanted to scream. I told him that he was acting like he wanted to be stuck in Kansas City for the rest of his life. "Your mom and I have even discussed moving to Texas," I said, "because it's really nice there." So, this was more than just a fun trip, I tried to explain; I wanted him to go see what it was like. Plus, his mom said she visited Texas often because his sister was there.

But Ah'Lee wasn't exactly keen on the idea. He said he wasn't moving out of Kansas City and didn't want to talk about it. So, I said I was still going on this trip to Texas. "It's already paid for," I reasoned, "and I want to see what it's like, so I'm going, even if you're not."

I tried to talk him into going, but he wasn't budging.

I was like, "Okay," but that wasn't the end of my mouth. No, I was hot. Ah'Lee didn't seem bothered by my mouth because on the two nights before we were supposed to leave, he came home and got in the bed like nothing had ever happened. He got under me like he always did. We would spoon and go to sleep, but eventually, he would turn away. However, these last couple of days before March 10, 2017, were a little different.

Ah'Lee was all over me. He would get right up on me and put his arms, legs, and any part of his body that he could on me. It was like we were a puzzle piece because every curve of my body he connected to his. Every movement I made, he made with me, and he held me all night—he wouldn't break the hold he had on me. This was different for him, but I wasn't complaining; I was loving every minute of it. Feeling his body heat and breath breathing on my neck gave me a sense of peace and relaxed me, so I was all in. I remember not wanting to get up to get the kids ready because it felt that good. It made me feel safe and secure. Not saying I didn't always feel safe, but it was something about his touch on these two nights that made it stand out.

The day before I was supposed to leave, I tried to find someone else to come with me, but nobody was available. I called a close friend of mine named Tanya and expressed my concerns to her and why I was upset. She understood, and I told her I was thinking about taking my kids with me instead of taking someone else. I asked if she could go, but she couldn't, so I said, "Forget it, that's okay, I'll just take my kids." She said that was a good idea. I talked to Tanya often about personal things, and she would always give me good advice, so when she said that, I knew it was good.

I went to pick up the rental car, but all they had was a small car that wouldn't fit all my kids. So, I decided it was a good time to take my car to the mechanic to get some things fixed that I'd been putting off; in that way, I could get a loaner car that I could drive to Texas. I remember thinking to myself that if it were meant for us to go, then they would give me something big enough for all of us.

When I dropped my car off, they ended up pulling around a big SUV for me. I was like, *"Okay, that works, so I guess it was meant to be."* So, the next morning my children and I were going to hit the road. Because I was still mad at Ah'Lee, I decided not to tell him we were leaving. I figured I would wait until we were already on the road to say "good-bye" so he wouldn't convince me to change my mind. However, I also decided I was going to write Ah'Lee a letter, letting him know how I felt about him not coming and about him figuring out what was more important: money or his family.

That night I got the kids all packed up as well as myself. Then I sat at the table and wrote the letter. At the time I was writing, I was working on pure emotion, but I should have prayed first; some of the things I wrote I should have explained better—why I was saying them, for instance. I don't remember what the letter said verbatim, so I won't speak on the details. Just know it wasn't that harsh but it just could have been a little more tactful—perhaps explained better with less emotion infused with my words.

❖ ❖ ❖

Have you ever done something without thinking before you did it? And then did your actions or words cause more harm than good? Did you wish you could take it back after you stopped being upset about whatever it was? Well, that's exactly how I felt on this day. If I had the chance, I would rewrite that letter. All my words in it would be totally different.

Tanika K. Judie

Share Your thoughts..........

13. ON THE ROAD

March 10, 2017

My alarm sounded, and after climbing out of bed, I woke the kids, telling them to get ready for school. I hadn't told them they weren't going to school because I wanted it to be a surprise —and I didn't want them to tell Ah'Lee and spoil it. The day before, Ah'Lee had made a comment, like he didn't believe I was really going to go anyway, so I had a trick for him. I didn't tell him I was getting up and leaving, and I didn't tell him the kids were going with me. So, while they were getting dressed, I went back to the room and laid back down with Ah'Lee for about 30-45 minutes.

When I was about to get up, I turned to face him. He was still sleeping and didn't notice I was looking at him. I laid there with my hand lying on his stomach and just stared at him. My hand raised up and down with every breath he took. His skin shimmered dark brown and oily, like always. He had just gotten a fresh haircut a few days before, so his face and hair were neatly lined up the way I liked it. His lips were slightly opened and moved a little with every breath he took. I laid there admiring him, trying to decide if I was going to have the guts to leave and not tell him. I laid there and thought about it for about five more minutes and thought to myself, *"I'm gonna teach him a lesson."* I moved in closer to him, put my hand on his neck— up close to the back of his head—and moved his head in close to mine. I put my lips on his and kissed him a couple of times until he woke up. He opened his eyes and looked at me the way he always did with those chestnut brown eyes, and then he lifted his head and kissed me back. We had this thing we always did when we kissed. We would kiss two times in a row, and then before I moved completely away, we would move back in and kiss again because third time was a charm. That was our thing.

I got up and started to get ready to go, and he went back to sleep. Before I walked out of the room," I leaned down and kissed Ah'Lee again and said, "I love you," and he opened his eyes and said he loved me, too. I lifted up, turned, and walked out the door.

When I got into the hall, my heart was beating fast. I had gotten really nervous all of a sudden. I went into the front room, got my purse where I had put the letter I'd written him the night before, grabbed the tape, and when the kids went outside to get in the car, I taped the letter to the back of the front door. I did that so that when Ah'Lee got up and walked in the front room, he would find it.

I closed and locked the door behind me, got in the car, and pulled out of the driveway. I remember calling my friend, Tanya, telling her I was leaving and that the kids were with me, and she said, "Good." After talking just a little while longer, we got off the phone and I hopped on the highway, going 435W. I drove to Walmart in Kansas and told the kids we were going to Texas; I told them we had to get some stuff for our drive. I also told them that we would stop and get some food before we started heading that way.

They were super excited. While I was at Wendy's, my phone started ringing. I looked down, and it was Ah'Lee face timing me. I pushed the button, but he called right back. I pushed the button again, and before I could put my phone down, he called again. By this time, I knew he had read my letter and was about to go off. I didn't want to answer because I also knew that he would try to talk me out of going, so I planned to wait—and just call him once we were on the highway.

But that didn't happen. As I stood there waiting for our food inside Wendy's, Ah'Lee kept calling, but this time he was calling straight through, not face timing me. I took a deep breath and answered the phone.

"Hello."

Ah'Lee said, "Why ain't you answering yo facetime, and where are you?"

I had to think quick. I said, "Answer when?"

Ah'Lee said, "Don't play with me, you saw me calling you."

I said, "I was trying to order some food."

He said, "Where are you?"

"I'm in Kansas."

Ah'Lee was so mad, I could hear it all in his voice. He said, "Tamika, don't play with me. Are you in Kansas? Where and with who?"

I said, "Ah'Lee, who else am I going to be with?"

He said, "Who are you out there with?"

"Ah'Lee, really?"

He said, "Okay, I see you playing," and he hung up in my face. I immediately texted him, saying he was tripping and thinking negative. I texted him, *"Who did you think I'm with? You're the one who should be with me,"* or words to that effect. Ah'Lee didn't text back, and I figured he wouldn't because he thought I was coming back to the house.

Well, I didn't. I got the food and marched to the car. The kids and I ate, and then we hopped on the highway. While driving past dozens of highway signs, billboards, and exit ramps, I remember thinking to myself, *"OMG, what did I just do? Ah'Lee is going to hate me for this."* Then another thought was like, *"Oh, well, if he would have come like he was supposed to, then we wouldn't be having this problem."*

While driving down the highway, I ended up finding out (I don't remember how) that one of my best friends, Tink, was reeling from a tragedy: the father of her son had been killed. I called her on the phone, and we cried together, and I tried my best to give my friend the best support I could over the phone. She was devastated, and my heart dropped; I felt so bad because I knew that she needed me, yet I was somewhere in Kansas and couldn't get to her. I was so sad that I couldn't be there for her, but I promised that I would be back soon, and I would be there with her as soon as I touched Kansas City again in a few days. We talked a little while longer, but then my phone lost its signal and dropped our call. I remember saying a prayer for my friend and made a mental note to call her back as soon as my phone got a signal.

While driving, I debated on turning around because I felt like my friend needed me, but something kept telling me to keep driving south, and I didn't want to let my kids down because they were now excited about our trip.

We kept driving but stopped a few times so my son could take pictures of the sky and the mountains. It was beautiful out there in no man's land. Even though we saw some pretty scenery on our drive, I kept thinking about Ah'Lee. He didn't call back, and I was wondering why and wondering what he was thinking. I remember calling my sister, Amber, telling her what I had done and telling her I was nervous. She asked why I was nervous, and I told her I didn't know. I told Amber I didn't know, but, on the inside, I did know.

I was nervous about Ah'Lee being mad at me and leaving our house. I was thinking that Ah'Lee was going to be gone when I got home to pay me back for leaving without telling him. I was thinking and nervous about all kinds of stuff. My mind started going crazy. I started thinking that Ah'Lee may get fed up and move out of our house, that Ah'Lee would leave me and go be with someone else. *"Yes,"* I said to myself, *"Go be with someone else."*

Some people may read that like, "Why would you say that?"

Well, the reason is because you just never know, and I know Ah'Lee wasn't perfect. He never disrespected me in our six years together, but that doesn't mean I put anything past him. Going back, I was nervous about my Buddy not wanting to be with me and saying, *"Forget you,"* since I did that. After driving and thinking, I knew he was mad, but most of all, I felt like he was hurt because I left and didn't say anything.

We kept driving, and I kept thinking. We made it to Oklahoma City, and then some crazy stuff started happening that made me contemplate turning around and going home, on top of me already being nervous about what Ah'Lee might do. I talked to Tanya again and told her my thoughts, and we were like, "Nah, just go." So, there we were on the road, driving for what seemed like days, and then we finally made it to Dallas.

The highways were super crazy, as well as the drivers not using blinkers; I ended up getting lost like four or five times and said to the kids, "If we don't find the hotel this time, we're turning around and going home." I was so irritated and tired from the drive—anything could have pushed me to go back home. Well, around 9:45 p.m., we made it to the room. Then we made a quick trip to the store, got swim stuff, and then went back to the hotel so the kids could swim.

I ended up texting Ah'Lee's sister, Tiffany, who lived there, letting her know the kids and I were in Texas. I also discussed some things I was thinking and feeling as far as her brother and I were concerned, and I told her that we were going to come to see her so we could talk and hang out. Around 10:30 or 10:45 that night, the kids and I left the room to go get some food. While sitting in the drive-through, my phone rang. I looked down, and it was Ah'Lee.

"Hello," I said cautiously, my heart in my throat.

He said, "Where you at?"

I said, "In Texas."

He said, "Aw, yeah, well, where the kids at?"

I said, "They're with me. I took them with me."

He said, "Aw, yeah, Tamika, what's that you on?" Then he hung up the phone before I could say anything else. I started to call him back but then told myself I would wait until I finished ordering the food and get back to the room.

However, I did text him. I don't remember everything I wrote, but I remember him texting back, "Yep."

I texted back, *Do you understand what I'm saying?* He didn't text back.

I texted and said, "Ah'Lee?"

He texted back, "Yeah." I figured he was still mad, so I just texted "I love you."

He texted, "I love you 2."

The kids and I ended up going back to the room to eat, and I got tired. I called Ah'Lee but he didn't answer. I called back a few times, and still no answer, so I texted him and told him something like, "I want you to know I love you . . . and I know you still mad . . ."

I can't remember what else I wrote verbatim, but he didn't respond to anything I said. After the last text, I said a silent prayer and went to sleep. I wish I would have tried to call him again or called back earlier, because little did I know that the text he sent saying, "I love you" was the last I would get from Ah'Lee, EVER!!

◆ ◆ ◆

Am I the only person who has ignored a call or text from a friend, partner, mom, dad, or someone you love and then never get to call or talk to that person again? If you have, how did it make you feel? Did you feel guilty? Did you feel regret? Did you feel like it was something you could have done to change, whatever it was that happened?

◆ ◆ ◆

I was all over the place, nervous about this man leaving

me—but not the possibility of him leaving me for good. I should have answered my facetime, and I should have just gone home, but if I did, would I have been able to change what took place at 2:30 a.m. the next morning? That's a question I often find myself asking God over and over again.

Tanika K. Judie

Share Your thoughts..........

14. THIS CAN'T BE REAL

March 11, 2017

Ring . . . Ring . . . I rolled over and glimpsed the cell phone, thinking it was Ah'Lee calling me back. But as my eyes adjusted, I saw that the phone read, Johnson Sister, Tasha. Searching my mind for why she might be calling me, I quickly pushed the side button to stop the ringing, knowing it will go to voicemail, and then I saw the time: 2:30 a.m.

"What could she possibly want this early in the morning?" my mind reeled, pushing me more fully awake, but then I quickly realized, "Maybe she's trying to see if her brother is with me."

Rolling back over, I adjusted my pillow, attempting to slip back into sleep. Just as I close my eyes, the mood is broken with another ring. Quickly glancing up, I saw that it was her again! For a split second I wanted to push the side button, but then decided I should probably answer—it wasn't like her to call in the middle of the night.

"Hello?" I gasped, trying not to sound alarmed.

"Tamika?"

"Yeah, what's up Tasha?"

Then instantly, her next words made my heart drop into my gut, taking my breath away.

"Ah'Lee got shot!"

I jumped up in a panic, barely able to breathe. "WHAT? Wait, he got shot, is he okay!?"

Through tears, the story spilled out . . . "Somebody tried to rob him, Tamika . . . and they shot him!"

"Tasha, is he okay?" I asked again, trying to stay calm. "Where did he get shot?"

"In the leg," she said.

I swallowed hard. "What part of his leg?"

From attending nursing school in the past and losing a friend to a gunshot wound to the leg, I knew that there's a main artery in your leg that can cause you to bleed out in seconds.

"I don't know," Tasha sobbed, "but they said he kept blacking out."

"No! I'm on my way," I say, "but . . . I'm in Texas."

When she told me he'd been blacking out, I know the bullet must have hit his artery. I hung up the phone and woke up my kids in a panic.

"GET UP, GET UP, WE HAVE TO GO!!!" I shook them all awake.

Sleep talking, they asked, "Why, mama?" At that moment my stomach felt empty and a burning knot was stuck in my throat as I tried to pull out the words, conveying the one thing I'd always dreaded . . .

"Ah'Lee got shot!!" I finally said, my voice now shaking.
My children began to ask questions. "Is he okay?"

The twins asked, "Mama, is Daddy okay?"

I looked at them with tear-filled eyes, and trying to remain calm I said, "I think so. We just have to get to him because he's waiting for us."

While the kids get dressed, I started packing our belongings; I feel as if time had stopped and I was moving in slow motion. I could feel my heart beating through my chest, much slower than normal. I couldn't breathe very well and could hear every shallow, labored breath.

Then suddenly, something told me to stop and pray. I immediately stopped, gathered my kids around me and held their hands. Then the words come tumbling out . . . the words I would soon regret praying. I know I will never forget this moment, this feeling, this deep angst . . . but will keep it in my heart forever.

"Dear God," I began, "I come to you now, asking you to protect Ah'Lee. I ask that you keep him safe. I ask that

you allow us to get home safely. Lord, I ask that you let your will be done in this situation. In Jesus name, we pray, Amen!"

The kids said, "Amen," and we grabbed their things and scrambled out the hotel door. Feeling like I was in a dream, I stopped at the desk to let them know I was checking out early. My clarity of mind surprised me. Yet opening the car door, I couldn't stop shaking and thinking about Ah'Lee. So many thoughts, fears, and hopes began swirling in my head.

Is he going to be okay? Is he up waiting on me? Is he looking for me? Is he thinking about me? Why did I leave? I need to be there by his side. Why am I not there when he needs me the most?

I was a wreck. Not knowing what to do, I was in a panic, trying to think of some way I could get home faster than the seven hours it took me to get to Texas from Missouri. While wracking my brain, I was also thinking about who I could ask to go to the hospital to let Ah'Lee know I was on my way and to wait on me. Every 30 minutes I tried calling his phone, but it always went straight to voicemail, fraying my nervous still more. My thoughts were frenzied. *"I simply must find someone to go talk to him and check on him!"*

I called my sister Tisha. When she answered, I tried my best to stay calm and tell her what happened. After managing to get it out, I asked, "Will you please go to the hospital and make sure he's okay and let him know I'm on my way?"

"Yes, yes, try to calm down," Tisha reassured me. "I'm going up there—I don't want you to get sick while you're on the road."

"Okay, thank you!" and we hung up the phone.

As I merged onto the highway, I felt like a ton of bricks was sitting on top of my chest, pushing my heart into my stomach. I felt numb and lost. All kinds of thoughts were spinning inside my head, but I told myself, *"Be cool, be cool, you've just gotta get home."* So, I turned the music on, grabbed the wheel with both hands, and pushed the gas down to the floor, letting my mind float away and zone out.

❖ ❖ ❖

Has your worst nightmare ever became your reality?? Have you ever felt like something ripped your heart out of your chest, and you still didn't die? I felt like I was a zombie from the time I got the call and still do at times.

Share Your thoughts..........

15. AUTOPILOT

"I have to get home and get to my husband!! I have to get home and make it to him, so he will know that I know, and he will fight!!" With my mind in "fight or flight mode," I kept repeating this over and over in my head throughout those long hours of driving, the whole time. I remember crying off and on, trying to play it off that I was okay, so the kids wouldn't see my fear and intense worry about Ah'Lee. I remember them asking me periodically, "Is Daddy okay?"

"Yes," I told them, "he's waiting on us to get there, so we just gotta get to him." I kept driving as fast as I could and trying not to think about the "what ifs." During this horrible time of limbo and nothingness, my phone was also ringing off the hook. I figured that everyone had found out that Ah'Lee had been shot and wanted to call and get info or tell me what was going on.

I was so mad and nervous that I wanted to answer and scream at everyone, but instead, I just hit "ignore." Then one time when my phone buzzed, I started to hit "ignore" but saw it was my sister Tisha. I quickly answered and braced myself for what she might say. *"Would she say he was still alive?. . or not? Or that he was in pain?"*

She said she was there but that the doctors weren't letting them know what was happening; it seemed the nurses were instructed to not tell them anything at that time. I remember asking her if she would let others know they should stop calling my phone because it was making me think the worst and making me nervous. So, my sister said she was going to post a message to Facebook and tell them to stop calling.

We hung up and I kept driving, yet I started feeling crazy. I remember feeling like something was leaving my body. It actually felt like something left me, and after that, I felt empty. I would describe the feeling as something like how the cartoon characters die—when you see their spirit lift and float off—that's exactly how I felt—like my spirit had left my body and I was just a shell driving.

I started feeling really sad, and I immediately felt like something was wrong, so I called my sister back. I asked Tisha if she had heard anything else, but she said, "No," and that she was going home; she had asked his mom to call her and let her know if anything changed.

I remember calmly asking, "Did he die, Tisha?"

"No, why are you saying that?" I heard her respond like she was in a different world.

I don't remember everything verbatim, but I told her that I could feel it, and I felt like she wasn't telling me the truth. I told her I was going to call her back and that I was calling his momma. I hung up with her, determined to get the real answer, and I dialed his mom's number.

She answered, and I asked her if Ah'Lee had died. "Have you talked to your sister?" his mom asked me, her voice sounding far away.

"Yeah, but she won't tell me nothing," I lamented. I remember his mom telling me to call my sister . . . and I don't remember what else she said but I said, "Okay," and hung up the phone.

Instead of calling my sister back, I called his sister Tasha.

"Tasha, tell me the truth, did he make it?" I asked her point-blank.

I don't remember her first answer, but what I do recall is begging her to tell me the truth. I told her I already knew because I had felt him leave me. Tasha got real quiet and finally said, "Yeah," so softly. She started crying and saying louder, "He's gone, my brother is gone, they killed my brother!!!"

Tasha was screaming at this point and could barely breathe.

I did my best to not cry myself . . . and I told her to calm down and asked who was with her. She didn't respond and I kept hearing screams in my ear.

I eventually hung up the phone and just left it lying in my lap. I glimpsed the road in front of me with tears stinging my eyes, a lump burning in my throat, and my heart beating so slowly, like one beat every two minutes, as I pushed hard on the gas.

I didn't know how to process the news. I looked over at my son now looking at me, and I started silently sobbing. He reached over, put his hand on my shoulder, and said, "It's okay momma."

I immediately had a flashback to Feb. 19, 2007, when I woke up crying and my son had jumped up and said, "It's okay, momma, I'll take care of you." This was after his father had been murdered—when he was just 5 years old and promising to take care of his momma—and now here we were ten years later, and he's 15 years old, again in the same position having to comfort his momma.

I snapped back to the present and cried harder, but this time not for me but for my son, for my kids, because they had just lost not only their mom's fiancé but the only father they had. All I kept thinking was, *"How am I going to tell them that he is gone?"*

I looked in the rearview mirror at the twins and Amya in the backseat, and just like I thought, they were looking right at me. I couldn't say a word, though, and had to wipe my face, telling myself, *"Just be cool Tamika, because they're in the car and you have to make it home."*

We ended up stopping after about an hour or so to get some gas and food and to use the restrooms. When I stepped out of the car, I felt like I was floating; I didn't know how my feet were moving, but they were.

I walked into the store, and on my way to the bathroom, I saw a purse that read, "THE JOY OF THE LORD IS MY STRENGTH! Nehemiah 8:10." I remember looking at that purse and almost passing out. I felt like Ah'Lee had put that there just for me. It was crazy, but I felt like that was him telling me that God was going to take care of me.

I just knew that was Ah'Lee giving me a message. I grabbed the purse and went to pay for it (and I still have it today). After using the restroom and paying for the gas, I walked over to Subway with the kids.

As soon as we ordered, I remember pulling Aaron to the side and telling him that Ah'Lee didn't make it. I told him and not the other kids because I felt like he was strong, and I needed him to help me because I wasn't okay. I remember him asking, "Momma, he didn't? He died?.. Where did he get shot at?"

I told him the details, and Aaron said, "Dang, momma! Dang, that's messed up."

My eyes welling with tears, I said, "Yeah, I know, son, but again..."

Aaron looked at me with tears in his eyes and said nothing; he just shook his head. I wiped my face, pulled myself together, and told the other kids to "come on," and within a few moments, we were back on the road.

Soon, as raindrops began pelting my windshield, I completely zoned out. I remember looking straight ahead, letting my natural driving instincts kick in as my mind checked out. I felt empty, I felt lost, I felt played, I felt guilty, I felt cheated, I felt hurt.

But most of all, I felt pain in my heart that made me feel physically sick. I felt like I couldn't breathe, so I cracked the window. I felt like I was going to pass out from time to time because my eyes kept getting extremely heavy, not from sleepiness but from almost blacking out.

I remember talking to a few of his close friends and his cousin, Terio, who talked and cried so much that I couldn't make out what he was saying. I told him I would call him when I made it to the city...I told him I loved him...and he told me he loved us and to drive safe.

After we hung up, I turned on the radio and hooked up my phone. All I could think about was Ah'Lee. I felt so much guilt for leaving and not facetiming him back, that it was making my head hurt. I kept saying in my head, *"I love you Ah'Lee . . . and I'm so very sorry."* I went through the playlist on my phone and played our favorite song, "You," by Toni Terry. When the song started playing, I started singing along softly along with the track, but then before too long, I found myself crying and screaming the words. I figured, *if I scream the words loud enough, Ah'Lee will hear me and maybe this nightmare will be over.* I was gone, though; I had forgotten I was driving. I remember closing my eyes and crying so hard, I felt like it was coming from the pit of my heart. Then I felt a hand on my shoulder, and I popped my eyes open, thinking I was waking from a dream . . . but it was my son rubbing my shoulder, asking me if I was okay and if I wanted him to drive.

I said, "I'm okay . . . really, I am . . . and I can keep driving."

The other kids asked me, "Momma, are you okay?"

And I said, "Yeah," although I couldn't gather enough courage to look up at them. I knew if I did, they would know the truth; my eyes would tell it all.

I tried to pull myself together, and I did a little, but I kept crying and shaking my head "no" because I wasn't going to accept this again. I was so mad and in shock, and I didn't know what to do.

The rest of the ride was a blur, except for when I heard sirens and didn't realize that they were for me. I had been staring straight ahead, looking at what seemed like nothing. I didn't see the road nor the cars in front of me, nor the police truck on the side of the road. I didn't even feel like I was driving . . . just floating.

I didn't feel my foot on the gas, nor did I feel my hands on the steering wheel. I had even forgotten that my kids were with me.

The sirens got so loud that I snapped out of my trans and looked up; then after looking around, I remembered I was driving and looked in the rearview mirror, spotting a white truck with flashing lights and sirens wailing.

I pulled over to the side, thinking the officer was going to go around me, but he didn't; he pulled over with me. I was like, *"Dang, I don't need this right now—I need to get home."* The cop came up to the window and asked me if I knew how fast I was going?

"No, officer, I'm sorry, I really don't."

He said, "You were doing 20 over the speed limit."

"Oh, no, I'm so sorry," I managed to say.

He asked," Where are you going in such a hurry?"

I told him about Ah'Lee, but not that he had passed; I told him I was trying to get home because he was shot. He asked to see my license and insurance and walked away. I was like, *"OMG, I'm going to jail."*

After about three minutes he came back, gave me my stuff, and said, "I'm going to cut you a break. I put that you were going 10 over the speed limit instead of 20. I need you to be safe and slow down because you'll be no good for him if you wreck and hurt yourself." I thanked the officer, took the ticket, and drove off. I thanked God for what the officer did and told myself to stay focused.

I kept driving and, once more, it started raining—which was an outdoor picture of how my insides were breaking. And the closer we got to the city, the harder the rain pounded on our car and in my heart. Thinking back on it a year later, on the same day, March 11, it rained again, and again I asked, *"Are those tears from Ah'Lee?"* This was the worst day of my life . . . and it was only going to get worse.

❖ ❖ ❖

Have you ever felt this kind of pain from any kind of loss in your life? A pain so bad that it felt like you had a hole in the middle of your chest where your heart used to be? How did you feel? What did you do? What were you thinking, or did you have any thoughts at all?

Share Your thoughts..........

16. SHATTERED

We finally made it back to the city, but before I did anything else, I had to return the loaner car to the dealership before it closed. I stopped at home and dropped off our bags so I wouldn't have to do anything but get my car when I got there. When I turned onto our block, it felt like I started moving in slow motion; I was pushing the gas, but the car was barely moving. I could see our house from the corner, and I remember looking down the street to see if Ah'Lee's car would be parked in the driveway, but it wasn't. Inching closer to the house, it seemed, my heart started skipping beats. Anxiety welled up inside, my palms turned sweaty, and I was actually afraid to pull up in the driveway. As the car seemed to turn itself into the driveway, I felt the emptiest feeling ever: like my heart hit my stomach, then my stomach hit my feet. I swallowed the biggest lump in my throat and put the car in park.

I told the kids, "Come on, let's put our stuff in the house."

I followed behind them, standing at the bottom of the stairs as Aaron unlocked the door. Fear gripped me as I thought about entering the home we had shared. I was finally able to lift my shoes and shuffle them forward, my feet moving like lead into the house. Tears began to roll down my face. I walked down the hallway to our room and stood at the door, my eyes darting to see if the bed was made or if anything was out of place, perhaps indicating that maybe, just maybe, he had come home, and it was all a prank.

However, everything looked as if it hadn't been slept on or moved. I dropped my bags and went back into the front room, asking the kids to go outside and that I was coming. As soon as they left out the house, it felt like my knees gave out, and I fell back on the couch. Crying hard now, I looked around at this once joyful house and shook my head. Peaking back inside, Aaron said, "You okay, momma?" I don't remember what I said exactly, but I know I told him, "No," and cried for a little bit, then got up and wiped my face . . . and we left the empty house. I remember thinking, *"This house will never be the same; how am I going to be able to stay here?"*

We dropped the car off, picked up my car, and headed to Ah'Lee's mom's house. On the way, I called my sister Tisha and asked if she would meet me there. Although she said "yes," I arrived there before her. Pulling up, I saw a lot of people outside, and I sat back on the seat and laid my head back, thinking, *"How am I about to tell the other kids that their father is dead?"* Tears rained from my eyes as I opened the door and, once more, told the kids to "come on."

I walked up to his mom's house, and the first person I saw was his auntie, Nita. I hugged her, we cried a little, and then I walked into his mom's house and headed up the stairs to the living room.

The sadness was so heavy in the house that I felt I was about to suffocate. I staggered to the top of the stairs, and I don't know who I made it to first, but we hugged as I screamed and broke down. I don't remember what all happened after that, but I know I was on the stairs trying to catch my breath and could barely see. I don't know where my kids were or how I managed to get up and make it to the den, but I did. I looked up and saw my sister and remember thinking, *"Thank God."* I told my sister, "We have to tell the kids." So, we gathered them with the help of Ah'Lee's mom and family and told them quietly that Ah'Lee had passed away.

The twins broke down crying and so did Amya.

Aaron cried, but he was more concerned about me, his brother and sisters, so he held it in. He was always like that. He would put his emotions to the side to care for me and them. That's one thing I love and hate about my son: he always puts us first and thinks about himself later, which has made him develop a wall in his heart and mind that's hard to tear down.

After we got the kids together, I believe we talked for a while, and then I remember his mom giving me the key to his car; I told her I would go get it and drive it to our house as I was the only one who knew where it was. You see, it was at the house of one of Ah'Lee's friends, and this young man only wanted me to come to his house to get it. He called me and said, "You can come, Tamika, but no one else." So, of course, I did just that.

The events from the rest of that day, I have to be honest and say, I don't remember at all. I know that a had a couple of seizures and ended up at my sister Ro's house because I didn't want to go home. I couldn't go back to that house that night; I needed to be around the people I loved because my true love was gone and was never coming back.

I do remember crying off and on all night. I even remember getting a text early the next morning, saying that my grand-dad (my dad's father) had just passed away. All I could do was cry even harder. Here I was, crying over my fiancé dying, and then the very next morning my granddad died, too. Talk about the worst events ever! I couldn't go be with my family, though, or even call because I couldn't get myself together. My heart had just been shattered double-time. *"What was I going to do now?"*

My life was bad, at least I thought that was it, but it only got worse.

◆ ◆ ◆

17. FUNERAL

After the medical examiner released his body, it was time to go to the funeral home to make funeral plans. Of course, Ah'Lee's family would go, but I wanted a close friend or sister by my side; I didn't know if I would be able to go and, most definitely, didn't want to go alone. My sister, Alisha, was always one to stay at my side. So, I called her and asked if she would go with me to make arrangements. To my relief, she said, "Yes." So now, as I tell this part of the story, please know I'm remembering everything the best I can because I was zoned out, and all was a little foggy.

We entered the room where the family was sitting and sat down ourselves. I remember his mother having my sister and I sit close to her. The room was filled with his sisters, aunts, and cousins. I remember seeing them all, but I was really on auto-pilot. I still couldn't wrap my head around the fact that we were about to plan my Buddy's funeral. This was all way too unreal.

Long story short, we looked over the book of flowers and caskets, and we picked a date to lay him to rest. I even shared some stories and videos that I had of Buddy. I shared with them that Ah'Lee had accepted Christ and gave them the date of this important decision. I shared with them about our reading the Word and praying together. It was a very sad day but looking at the videos and pictures made us smile. I shared things with the family that they didn't know about Ah'Lee; well, another side of him that he didn't show other people. It was amazing. The family was able to see videos of Ah'Lee being funny, and him with a look of love in his eyes and on his face.

Ah'Lee was special, and regardless if people, believe it or not, he was sweet—with a big heart—and he loved hard. He loved really hard in the way he knew to love, and when he loved you, there was no getting out of it; that, we both had in common. We would fight for the ones we said we loved and wouldn't let them go. Which sometimes was a bad thing.

After the hard part was over, we were able to go see him. I knew I wasn't ready, but I had to do it. I wanted to see him for many reasons: first, because I wanted to see if he looked peaceful or not; next, I wanted to see if he looked like himself; and last, I wanted to make sure this was real, that I wasn't dreaming. I wanted to know if the love of my life was really gone. I felt like I was going to be strong, but on the inside, my body was saying "no!"

My sister was with me the whole time. We walked through the doors, and I remember going very slow, taking deep, slow breaths, and peeking around the other people to see if he was really lying there. I remember having to stop a few times, but I was determined to see if it were true. We got closer, and I remember seeing the color purple. I stopped and took a deep breath and went closer . . . but after that, everything went black. The next form of light I saw was when I woke up in the hospital; I was told I had had a seizure.

I remember being upset at myself because I didn't get to see him, but I was told that I did see him. However, I couldn't remember anything . . . only something purple. His mother and sister came into the hospital room, and we talked. While our conversation was hazy, they did tell me I saw him. I felt so bad, though, because I didn't believe them or anybody else who said I did because I would have remembered. I cried and begged for them to take me back. I felt so empty and broken, I didn't know what to do. I remember his sister, Tiffany, telling me that I kissed him and then touched my mouth to see what I had felt. I had touched my lips and they were cold, and she said that's because I had kissed him on the lips. At this, I cried even harder. I asked how he looked, and they said he looked good. I was crushed because I kept closing my eyes trying to remember his face, but I saw nothing. It hurt me all over again because what I was looking for—the chance to see him, to look into his beautiful face and know that this was real—I didn't get . . . and it was all due to having a seizure. Yes, I would still get to see him in the casket at the funeral, but somehow, I felt cheated out of seeing him right then, when everything was so deeply raw and I craved with my whole being to see and hold him.

Still, after that day, we continued to get things ready for his home-going celebration. I was able to select his clothes for the funeral, and I was honored to do it. I knew he was very picky about what he wore and loved to match head to toe, including his underwear and right down to his socks. I wanted to get Ah'Lee something black, as that was his favorite color as well as mine, but everything I found wasn't good enough for him. I finally came down to his next favorite color, blue. I was able to find him a blue polo button-down shirt, khaki polo pants, a white V-neck t-shirt, black polo underwear, black polo socks, and black polo glasses.

I said, "Perfect, this is how he would do it." After purchasing everything, I took it all home and sprayed his clothes down with one of his colognes that I loved for him to wear. I put his clothes in a bag and tied them tight to hold in the smell. I dropped off the clothes at the funeral home, then went back to get the children, and I ready for this day as well. I ended up getting us all the same outfit I had gotten for Ah'Lee: blue polo shirt and khaki polo bottoms. I also told the pallbearers where they could find the exact same outfit that Ah'Lee was wearing, and they all went and got it so that everyone could match him.

The day before the funeral, we were able to go see Ah'Lee and make sure everything was done to our liking. I remember walking down the aisle to see him—with my sister, Alisha, at my side, and I was praying. She was in my ear praying, too, and continually encouraging me. I kept hearing the song "Free" in my head, and I said, *"Okay, I know; I know he's free, I know."* I was able to make it to see Ah'Lee, and this time I had the strength to actually see him and talk to him. My first thought was *"You look amazing baby!"* I was so happy that he looked like himself; he just looked asleep. He was as clean as a whistle, and everything was perfect. I knew he would have been pleased. I still can see his face in my head from that day. He looked so good, all I could do was cry and smile. I was sad, but deep down I was truly happy that he was in heaven and not going through life or hell no more. Only thing was, he left us—me and his kids.

March 18, 2017

"Today is the day!!!" I said in my head. I remember opening my eyes from about one or maybe two hours of sleep. I didn't want to move, but I knew I had to.

NOTE: This day was very foggy, so bear with me!!

I finally made myself get up, then got the kids up and told them to get dressed. I remember turning on gospel music and taking my medicine because I knew this day was going to be harder than ever. All I kept thinking was, *"This is it ... This is the last day I will ever get to see my Buddy physically. This is real!! I'm about to bury the love of my life, my soul mate, my kids' father, my best friend. I can't do this!! How am I going to do this?"* I stopped and sat on my bed with my head in my hands, and said, *"I can't do it. I'm not going to make it."* My heart was pounding in my chest harder than ever before. I had to take slow, deep breaths so I wouldn't pass out. I felt weak, dizzy, and just exhausted. I forced myself to stand up and said, *"You have to do this."* So, I put the little energy I had into gear and got ready. A little while later, my family and Tracy (ZaMayah's mother) arrived at my house. I got Stink dressed, did her hair, and sat on the couch. Sitting there for a second, I started crying and said, *"I'm not going. I can't do this!!! My husband is really gone."* I looked around at the people in the house that Ah'Lee and I once shared, and I got mad. I was mad because not one person in the house understood my pain. Not one person in the house knew what I was dealing with on the inside. At that moment, I needed one person to feel it with me and tell me they knew what I was going through, and I didn't have that. I was also sad because the funeral of my best friend's son's father was on the same day, at the same time, and I couldn't be there for her, and she couldn't be there for me. I felt for her more because she had lost two people—him and Ah'Lee; Ah'Lee was her friend from their neighborhood. At that moment, while I sat there crying and looking around, I felt more alone than I had felt during this whole process. Yet this was just the beginning.

I would rather not go into detail about his homegoing celebration, but I will say that it was beautiful, sad, emotional, and anything else you could think of a funeral to be. Ah'Lee went out in style, just like he would have wanted. That day was very draining, and to leave him at the cemetery was the hardest thing for me and my children to do. I thought this day was hard, but it was the first day of the worst days of my life!!

❖ ❖ ❖

Normally, I would end a chapter with a question, but this time I won't. *This time I just want you to think about a time where you had to do something you never thought you would have the strength to do.* You can write it down but if you don't want to write it, that's fine, just think about it. I would also like for you to prepare your mind for the chapters to come, as one of them will be straight from my journals. What you will soon read—after the next chapter—is directly from the days when I could pick up a pen or pencil and write. Wait, there will be more memories, but I want to make sure you see that this is as real as it gets.

"DON'T JUDGE ME I LOVE GOD, BUT I DID A LOT OF CUSSING AND FUSSING AT HIM."

◆ ◆ ◆

YOU'VE BEEN WARNED, BUT PLEASE READ ON BE-CAUSE THIS IS THE BEGINNING OF DELIVERANCE!!!

18. EMPTY

I was devastated about the love of my life, my other half, leaving me. I didn't know what to do, what to say, where to go, or how to think—about anything else but him. I used to scream so loud, the pain so raw and unbearably sharp, and that's all I could do. It felt like my insides were being pulled down to the pit of my stomach, with someone kicking me in the gut—hard. I couldn't stop thinking about the fact that, yet again, I had lost another person I loved. Yet, this time was different: he was my soulmate, my fiancé, my best friend, and a father to our children.

I thought, *"Now I'm back at square one, but why? Why did God do this to me if He loves me so much?"* I was so hurt and heartbroken that I felt empty like I had nothing in my body. I was weak. I couldn't eat for days. I went without using the bathroom for days. It was like I couldn't do anything at all.

I was scared to sleep in my bed when I got home because Ah'Lee wasn't there to protect me. He wasn't there to hold me. He wasn't there to wake me up or help me when I had a seizure in my sleep. I was all alone! I was mad at God for allowing me to feel this much pain and not help me feel better. I would call and beg my cousin, Andre, to come over and sit with me and the kids until we could fall asleep. I would lay on the couch and talk to him, his daughter's mother Monica, and his daughter. They would stay for hours if we needed them to. I would lay in Ah'Lee's hoodie, cover up my head, and eventually fall asleep— and then Andre and Monica would sneak out.

I would have dreams that would wake me up because all I saw was my husband fighting for his life. I would see him falling and bleeding everywhere. It got so bad that I would wake up and force myself to not go back to sleep. Andre, Monica, and the baby would spend the night with us sometimes, just so they could make sure we were okay. Monica would even come and go places with us so we would be happy. They were a blessing to us and still are to this day! I love them so much and wouldn't change our relationship for anything in this world. Andre still protects us, makes sure we are okay, and loves on us whole-heartedly. We thank God for him.

But going back . . . My heart was empty; I told myself I didn't want to love anybody again because they always die. I felt like I was the reason why. Like I was cursed. I would ask God why this had happened to me, but He wouldn't answer.

I don't remember the exact day, but a good friend of mine called and told me to come by because she wanted to give me something. When I got there, she handed me a box that had a journal, a couple of candles, a t-shirt, a pen, and a small notepad. She told me to write everything down. I said okay, but I didn't want to write or do anything because I was mad and had noth-ing to say. We talked a little longer and then hugged, and I left. I went home, sat on the bed, and forced myself to write . . . and this is all I managed to get out:

The new chapter in my life

Devastation, Tragedy, loss, Heart-break, alone, loneliness, Anxiety, Anger, screaming

Everything that goes on in my mind

Damn Here I go again

Lord Please Help Me!!

Journal Entry:

The new chapter in my life.

Devastation, Tragedy, love, Heart Break, alone, loneliness, Anxiety, Prayer, Screaming.

Everything that goes on in my mind.

Damn, Here I go again.

Lord, Please Help Me!!

After scrawling those few words, I put the journal down because I didn't want to write anything else—yet my mind kept going back to a conversation that Ah'Lee and I had had about me writing a book and starting a blog, as well as setting up a Facebook page to promote them both. Ah'Lee had supported and encouraged anything I wanted to do. He told me that he would pay for anything I needed to get the book published. As my biggest supporter and #1 fan, he always pushed me to do more and accomplish my goals . . . so when he passed, I simply didn't want to write anymore; I just couldn't do it.

So, after making my first feeble attempt, I pushed the journal halfway under the bed—I didn't want to see it or touch it, so I didn't. I was sad and tired of crying, so I finally decided to lay down in bed. I just laid there. I put my head under the covers and closed my eyes—and stayed right there in bed for a week or longer. I didn't get up to eat, drink, shower, brush my teeth, or even use the bathroom. I was dehydrated, but I didn't care. I felt paralyzed, and I couldn't move. It was like something very big and oppressive was weighing me down.

When I think back to that time, I can't believe how depressed I was. Some people may not believe that I didn't use the bathroom, but I had nothing in me to come out. I felt like my bladder had stopped working, literally. My mouth was dry; it felt like it was stuffed with cotton . . . and above all else, I didn't care . . . and just kept lying there. My head was all over the place and I couldn't make it stop. My children came in and out, but I couldn't function. I couldn't be there for them at that time, and I knew they were sad, but there was nothing I could do. I couldn't help myself, so I most definitely couldn't help them. I was drowning in sorrow, hurt, rejection, pain, and resentment. I felt horrible, my heart was broken, and I could physically feel the pain—like I couldn't breathe like a knife was piercing my chest like I had fallen into a deep, dark pit that I couldn't scale . . . and nothing would make the agony go away.

Before his funeral, I had met his Aunt Frances. One day we were on the phone talking, and she said, "I'm not going anywhere; you are stuck with me."

I'm thinking in my head, *"Yeah, right . . . everybody says that, and then after the funeral, everyone forgets."* Well, she didn't. She called me daily, but I wouldn't answer the phone because I didn't want to hear anything positive; I felt like it was all a lie. God hurt me, and I didn't want to hear anything about Him. I didn't want to hear anything—I just wanted to be mad and be left alone. I was so sad one day and going crazy in my head, I just wanted to die. Finally, I had enough—and I forced myself to get up out the bed—because, at that point, I was just done.

I started talking to God and said, "Take me now, I'm tired of this pain, and I'm done." I wanted the pain to stop, and I figured the only way to do it was to end it all. So, I decided that I was going to do it that day and leave my children and everybody else alone. I wasn't helping the kids or talking to anybody anyway. The kids were at school, so it was the perfect time to get it done. I walked out of my room, weak and exhausted, but managed to make it to the kitchen. I went to the place where I kept my pills and looked around for my daily medicine and for any other pills I could take. I found my pills and some extra ones, got some water, poured all the pills into my hand, took a drink of the water, and threw all the pills into my mouth. I swallowed the mouthful of pills, set the cup down, and walked back to my room and got into bed. I laid there and waited to die.

I felt like if I died I would get to be before God and talk to Him; I had a lot of questions for Him and He had some explaining to do. I ended up falling asleep after lying there for what seemed like forever. I don't remember what happened after that, but clearly, I didn't die because I'm here now writing this book.

I was so mad!! I couldn't stand God. Why didn't he take me home like I asked him to? Not only was I mad at God, but I was even mad at Ah'Lee, too, because he didn't come and get me or come and tell me why he left. My devastation had merged with bitterness, self-pity, and inward rage. I didn't know what else to do, so I seized the one thing I said I wouldn't ever pick up again—the journal my friend gave me—I grabbed a pen, and I started to write.

At times we want to be in control of if we live or die, but God is in control of it all. When I woke up after attempting to kill myself, I was seething with anger. I wanted to curse God for not coming to get me.

❖ ❖ ❖

Have you ever tried to take your life into your own hands and failed? Did you ever stop to think that God blocked it for a purpose?

Share Your thoughts..........

19. THIS IS LIFTED DIRECTLY
FROM MY JOURNAL

These journal entries are not in order as far as the dates are concerned.

In these journal entries, you will see the raw emotion that I was feeling at the time. One minute I was up, one minute I was down, I was angry, I was sad, I was disappointed, I was helpless, screaming/crying out to God for help, I was blaming myself, God, Buddy and just all over the place. Please brace yourself as there will be some foul language and a lot of other craziness. I wanted to leave it as it was (not edited or anything) so there are some names that are left as actual names. This is not everything, but this is where it all started. Here goes nothing....

Journal Entry: 3-25-17

I'm on an emotional rollercoaster!! This is all so crazy. I'm happy for him but sad he left me. Happy he's free and with God but wish I could still see him. UGH!! My feelings are all over the place. God please step in and fix me!!

BUDDY, I MISS YOU SO SO MUCH!! I HAVE THIS FEELING! NO WARNING, NO I LOVE YOU, NO GOODBYE. You didn't even text me back after I expressed my feelings to you. You could have at least texted me and said ok or something. I got nothing Ah'Lee. It's not fair. It's not fair you just upped and left me no answers, no plan, just gone. You know how I am and what I've been through. Why wouldn't you talk to me? You felt it Ah'Lee, I know you felt something. The days before you held me different. You connected with my body like a puzzle piece. You've never done that before. So you knew something wasn't going to be the same. You could have helped me in some way. You always used to. I CAN'T BELIEVE THIS HAPPENED AND YOU JUST LEFT ME WITH NO WARNING OR ANYTHING! I'm SO MAD AT YOU but I miss you so much. I love YOU SO MUCH, BUDDY!

God, you let the other man die? Why? I'm sorry God but I wanted to live so he would go to jail. I can say I'm disappointed. SMH!!

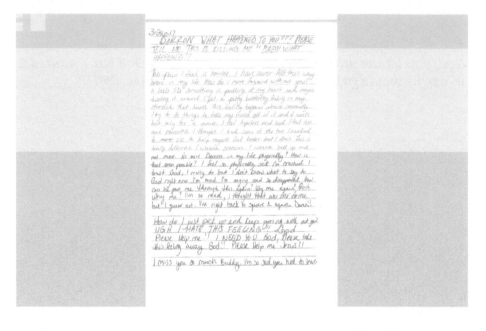

Journal Entry: 3-26-17

AH'LEE WHAT HAPPENED TO YOU??? PLEASE TELL ME. THIS IS KILLING ME!! BABY WHAT HAPPENED??

This pain I feel is horrible. I have never felt this way before in my life. How do I move forward without you? It feels like something is pulling at my heart and maybe twisting it around. Get a pity feeling in my stomach that hurts. This feeling happens almost constantly. I try to do things to take my mind off of it and it works but only for a minute. I feel hopeless and sad. I feel lost and powerless. I thought I had some of the tools I needed to use to help myself feel better but I don't. This is totally different. I wanna scream. I wanna ball up and not move. No more Ah'Lee in my life physically? How is that even possible? I feel so physically sick. I'm crushed. I trust God, I really do but I don't know what to say to God right now. I'm mad. I'm angry and so disappointed. How can he put me through this again? Why me again? God, why me? I'm so mad, I thought that was over for me but I guess not. I'm right back to square 1 again. Damn!!

How do I just pick up and keep going without you? UGH, I HATE THIS FEELING!! God, Please Help me!! I NEED YOU, GOD, Please take this feeling away God!! Please Help me, Jesus!!

I miss you so much, Buddy. I'm so sad you had to leave.

Journal Entry: 3-26-17

<u>*My Struggles*</u>   <u>*Scriptures to Match Struggles*</u>

Hurt   John 16:33
   Pain   1 Peter 4:12-19
   Anger   Colossians 3:8, 12-13
  Sadness   Psalm 3:3
Lonely   Isaiah   43:1
Understanding   Jeremiah 33:3
Lost   Psalm 34:18
Depression   Psalm 27:14
Grief   Isaiah 55:4
Heart Broken   Psalm 147:3
Strength   Psalm 71:20

Journal Entry: 3-27-17

Good Morning buddy, I love you and miss you so much.
God, Please help me have a better day then I did yesterday. Please touch my mind and my heart. You said you wouldn't leave me. You said to ask you and you'll give it to me. You said cast my cares on you. I give it to you God!! Please help me. I can't do this without you. Please show me what to do God. What is it you want me to do? I am yours. Help Me!

I feel better then I did earlier. I went and handled some business. Listened to some encouraging music and set over my sister Ro house for a while. I decided to set a small goal to take it minute by minute then increase

to hour by hour when time allows and go from there. I will be fine.
God is going to get me through this. He told me he would and I trust
him so I know he will. He said his word cant come back to him void.
So, God, you said you would never leave me nor forsake me and I'm
counting on you!!

Lord, I thank you for this day and all the amazing people in my life.
Thank you for blessing me with an amazing support system at this
time. Can you please tell Ah'Lee I love him and would like to see him
in my dreams. Tell him I miss him so much and wish that he could
come home to sleep with me, and just hold me again. However, I
know he's happy and he's with you and I wouldn't trade him being
with you for my own happiness or selfish reasons. I love you Lord
and thank you again. Amen!!

I LOVE YOU AND MISS YOU BUDDY!! I think of you constantly.
Wish I could hug you and tell you I love you again. Missing my baby

so much!!

It's crazy how things work. One minute you think you have accepted the that he's gone and the next your right back stuck wishing he would come back home. I hate the roller coaster, but I know it's all part of the process and Ah'Lee wouldn't

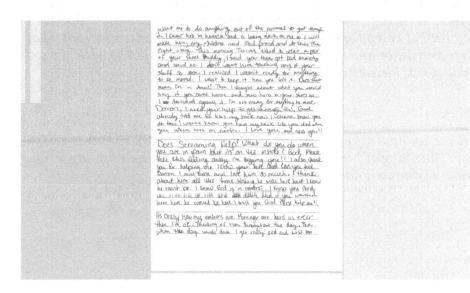

want me to do anything out of the normal to get through it. I know he's in heaven and is looking down on me so I will make him, my children and God proud and do this the right way. This morning Terion asked to wear a pair of your shoes Buddy, I said yea then got bad anxiety and said no. I don't want him touching any of your stuff so soon. I realized I wasn't ready for anything to be moved. I want to keep it how you left it. Does that mean I'm in denial? Then

121

I thought about what you would say if you come home and saw him in your shoes so I decided against it. I'm not ready for anything to move. Ah'Lee, I need your help to get through this. God already told me he has my back now I wanna know you do too. I wanna know you have my back like you did when you were here on earth. I love you and miss you!!

Does Screaming Help? What do you do when you are in pain but it's on the inside? God, Please take this feeling away. I'm begging you!! I also thank you for helping me. I know you're here God can you tell Ah'Lee I miss him and I love him so much. I think about him all the time. Wishing he was here but I know he can't be. I know God is in control. I know God is in control. I know you God are in control of life and death and if you wanted him here he would be here. I trust you, God. Please help me!!

It's crazy how my emotions are. Mornings are hard as ever then I'm ok. Thinking of him throughout the day. Then when the day winds down I get really sad and miss him more than I did earlier in the day. I guess I wake up to reality, ponder on it during the day and it hits me like it just happened all over again at night! I HATE THIS FEELING. God doesn't make mistakes I can't forget that but man I wish this one could be undone. Rewind and it never happened. I want more time, but do I need more time? Would more time only make me feel worst? IDK, I just know I miss my baby A LOT!!

GOD WHAT DO YOU NEED ME TO DO, TELL ME!!!! Please tell me, God!! I'M ALL IN GOD, I'M IN!!

If only I could call Heaven and talk to you, Buddy. I just want to *know you are not mad at me. I want to know that before you left you forgave me for leaving. I just want to know that we are cool. I want to know that we were still in love! I wanna talk to you and see your smile and hear that funny laugh. If only I could for 1 last time. Would I wanna let go? Probably not but I would be happy. I be thinking all kinds of things. I wish we could have communicated better. I wish you would have opened up just a little more. It's ok though some things are better without knowing. I just pray that you forgive me for all the things I did wrong. I want you to know how I feel about you. I wish I would have told you how I really felt about the person I knew you was. I know you know now. I love you, Buddy! Forever and Ever Missing my baby!!*

Journal Entry: 3-29-17

Hey, my Buddy, I miss you so much. I love you and think about you all the time. I hate being here without you here with me. I know you wouldn't have left me if it was up to you. I just pray you weren't mad at me. I wasn't trying to hurt you. I just wanted you to realize you really wanted your family. I'm so sorry for leaving you. It wasn't on purpose. I would never hurt you like that. Now I'm without you. Ugh, it hurts. Well, Buddy until I see you again please protect us and watch over all of us. Loving and missing you!!

God, please mend my Broken Heart!! Fill all the empty spaces in my body!! Heal my children's broken hearts, mend them together and make their broken hearts whole again. Please God give me the strength I need to get through this and to help my children. They need me and I want to be there for them and to be present with them not just physically but mentally. I know you can and will do it, Lord. You said you have me. You will carry me if you have too. You said I can do all things through Christ that strengthens me. I believe it and I receive it. I thank you in advance for what you are going to do for me and my children. In Jesus name, Amen!

THY WILL BE DONE!! JESUS!!!

I LOVE YOU AND MISS YOU SO MUCH, BUDDY!!

so he called you back home. I'm sad but happy you are back with him. I'm even happier to know I will be there with you and God one day. And we will get to be together again. I just have one favor. Can you continue to be my light while I'm here? My path gets dark sometimes and I need a light to guide me. Will you please continue to be that for me Buddy? I pray the answer is yes. I love you and thank God for the time we were able to share. I miss you so much!!

I MISS You and Love You so much Buddy!!

God, can you please come in and renew me. Touch my heart, my mind and my spirit. I need you. I'm inviting you into my body. Please help me. I love you!!

God, Please help me with the guilt I feel for leaving Damon and going to Texas. Lord please help my mind. I need you! I love you! Amen!

I Love you too Damon Blackmon! I got your message! I know that was from you. I really needed that. I looked at my phone I saw Ash's name but when I opened my phone all I saw was Blackmon and I love you! I know you made it read that way. Man that just made my day. I remember getting Ash's text all the time. I love you So much baby And miss you I know that was you letting me know you love me and part of me says you want me to know you are not mad.

127

Why can't this be a dream?? I hate that this is real. I miss my Buddy! I love you Buddy and miss you! Goodnight!

Journal Entry: 3-30-31

Good morning God and Buddy! I just wanted to say I love you so much and miss you like crazy. You were my only love here on earth. No matter what you or I did we loved each other, and I wouldn't have changed the love we shared for anything. I love you again my Buddy! God thank you for sharing him with me for as long as you did. I love you!

Buddy, I had to tell the LINC lady about what happened to you and it tore me apart. But as I was talking to her it came to me. I told her you wasn't perfect but you was our perfect. Meaning you weren't perfect to the world or for the world, but you were perfect for us. For our family. You were our knight in shining armor. We loved you so much. Buddy, you helped God. I say that because when I met you, I was in a dark place. God used you to lead me out of that place and make me happy. You lead me to the light Buddy. Then God used me to help you come back to his light because you lost your way. We were a blessing from God to each other. However, your work was done so he called you back home. I'm sad but happy you are back with him. I'm even happier in knowing I will be there with you and God one day. And we will get to be together again. I just have one favor; can you continue to be my light while I'm here? My path gets dark sometimes and I need a light to guide me. Will you please continue to be that for me, Buddy? I pray the answer is yes. I love you and thank God for the time we were able to share. I miss you so much!!

I miss you and Love you so much, Buddy!!

God, can you please come in and renew me. Touch my heart, my mind, and my spirit. I need you. I'm inviting you into my body please help me. I love you!!

God, please help me with the guilt I feel for leaving Ah'Lee and going to Texas. Lord, please help my mind, I need you! I love you! Amen!

I love you too Ah'Lee Johnson! I got your message. I know that was from you. I really needed that. I looked at my phone I saw Tasha's name but when I opened my phone all I saw was Johnson and I love you! I know you made it read that way. Man, that just made my day. I remember getting those text all the time. I love you so much baby and miss you. I know that was you letting me know you love me and part of me says you want me to know you are not mad

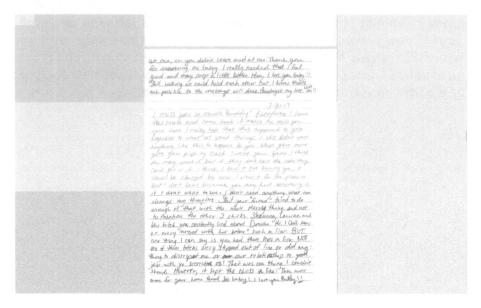

At me, or you didn't leave mad at me. Thank you for answering me, baby. I really needed that. I feel good and may sleep a little better. Man, I love you baby!! Still wishing we could hold each other but I know that's not possible so the message will due. Goodnight my love. Love you!!

Journal Entry: 3-31-17

I miss you so much, Buddy! Every time I leave this house and come back it makes me miss you even more. I really hate that this happened to you. Regardless of what we went through I still didn't want anything like this to happen to you. When your mom gets your property back, I want your iPhone. I think she may want it but if they don't have the code, they can't get in it. I think I know it but knowing you, it could be changed by now. I want it for the pictures, but I don't know because you may have something in it, I don't want to see. I don't need anything that can change my *thoughts. Sh*t your "friend" tried to do enough of that with the whole bm thing and not to mention the other 3 chicks. Shawnna, Lauran, and the chick you constantly lied about Donisha. "Mr. I don't know or ever messed with her before!" Such a liar. But one thing I can say is you had them chicks in line. NOT ONE of them chicks ever stepped out of line or did anything to disrespect me or our relationship so good job with yo secretive butt!! That was one thing I couldn't stand. However, it kept the chicks in line. They never came to your home. Good job baby! I love you, Buddy!!*

Journal Entry: 4-1-17

Good morning God, I just want to say I love you and I want to thank you for my life. I want to thank you for my children's lives and for choosing us again to have life. I want to thank you for my Buddy and all the time you allowed us to share. I thank you for saving both of our lives and loving us unconditionally. You are amazing God. To my Buddy, I love you and miss you like crazy. Words can not express the love I have deep in my heart for you. I'm happy for you but it's hard to show it because I'm also sad it was time for you to go. The kids and I weren't ready. We wanted more time, but I know God has the last say and knows what's best for you and for us. So, baby again I'm happy for you and excited to get to see you again one day. You are my inspiration and I know now that I can get there and be like you and be with you. I lobe you so much my Buddy!!

I miss you, my Buddy! Not a minute goes by that I'm not thinking about you.

Wishing you were here or coming back. I love you! P.S. tell me what you think about me being close to our cousin? Is it cool or do you want me to stay away from him? I'll be waiting on your answer Buddy. I love you again!! R.I.H. (rest in heaven).

Buddy, I love you and miss you so much. I wish I could see you and talk to you. Touch you and hold you. My thoughts are racing, and I need you to help me slow them down. I just wish I knew you would be coming home. Wishful thinking!! I love you and miss you!

I love you Buddy, Goodnight Baby!! I miss you!! Lord, I need you. Please show up and show me you're here. I love you so much, God!! I'm desperately waiting on you, God!

Journal Entry: 4-3-17

Buddy, I love you so much. I miss you so much!! I pray you are not upset with me. I just be needing people around to feel better. I know you probably hate it. I pray you're not upset. I love you again.

Lord, please walk with me on this day I need you like never before. I trust you and I won't move without you!!

God, I need you so much right now. I need your guidance, your love, your strength, and your peace. I can't do this or anything else without you, God!! Help me please God. I need you more now than ever before. I want to do whatever it is you have for me to do. But God please take the pain away, the depressed feeling, the lonely feeling, the sad feeling, and the bad feeling away from me. Take away and remove from me any anxiety, fears, and sickness away God. I know you can. I need you, God. I'm desperate for your presence God. Come in and restore my soul, my mind, clean my heart, God. Renew my spirit oh God!! I know that only you can help me. Help me to become the woman of God you created me to be. In Jesus name, Amen!

I love you and Miss you Buddy! P.S. If I never told you why I called you "Buddy" here's the reason. When we were coming up they had this doll called Buddy, it was a song that came on the comercial. My Buddy My Buddy, where ever I go he's gonna go my Buddy and some other words. But you were my favorite Man, They etc. I knew you would always be by my side. Love ya!

7-5-17

Good morning my Buddy, Sorry I didn't write you yesterday. I wasn't feeling good. Kamora and Asia came over and stayed with me all day. It made me so happy. Like you was here taking care of me. I'm so thankful for them. Also Marely is going to let pink come and stay with me. She also said she could move out of town with me to texas. I hope you are happy about that. I am! Well I love you Buddy and miss you so much!!

Dear Dad, I love you and I thank you for this day. I thank you for waking me up and getting me out of bed a little bit this yesterday. I want to ask you is it your will for me to change my last name to Blackwell? I really want to, my heart says yes but I wanna know what you want me to do. Please give me your answer. Also Zaahiyah mom said she can come and live with me. What do you think? Is that a good idea? I really want her to be raised right. So I know you will provide for us. I love you and miss you Amen.

135

Tanika K. Judie

I love you and miss you, Buddy! P.S. if I never told you why I called you Buddy here's the reason. When we were coming up, they had this doll called Buddy. It was a song that came on the commercial. My Buddy, My Buddy, Wherever I go he's gonna go my Buddy and some other words, but you were my favorite man, toy, etc. I knew you would always be by my side. Love you!

Journal Entry: 4-5-17

Good Morning my Buddy. Sorry I didn't write you yesterday. I wasn't feeling good. Momma and Tasha came over and stayed with me all day. It made me so happy. Like you was here taking care of me. I'm so thankful for them. Also, BM is going to let Stink come stay with me. She also said she could move out of town with me to Texas. I hope you are happy about that. I am! Well, I love you Buddy and miss you so much!!

Dear God, I love you and I thank you for this day. I thank you for waking me up and making me feel better than yesterday. I want to ask you is it your will for me to change my last name to Johnson? I really want to; my heart says yes but I wanna know what you want me to do. Please give me your answer. Also, Stinks mom said she can come and live with me. What do you think? Is that a good idea? I really want to raise her. If so, I know you will provide for us. I love you and need you. Amen.

I went to see "The Shack" today and I would have to say it was outstanding. It had everything in it I needed to hear. God is so good. I've been wanting to see this movie since before Ah'Lee passed away and now I'm glad I had to wait because it was right on time. I felt like God was talking to me. It was awesome. I have to get to the root of my issues; I have to go through the pain of this loss, I have to forgive myself for leaving Buddy and going to Texas, I have to forgive other people who have hurt me in my past and forgive myself from mistakes I made in my past. I have to allow God to come in and heal me, I have to live and be there for my children and not let the pain and sorrow consume me. I have to step out on faith and trust God. I know that God is with me every step of the way. He will never leave me. I have to go through this process and not build a wall up and shut God out. I have to forgive the people who took my children's fathers away as well as the people/person who did this to my Buddy. I know that Heaven is real, and Buddy is ok. I know that he can see me, and he is not mad at me he

Tanika K. Judie

forgave me. I have to eventually let him go when I get through this process so he can be free. And so, I can be free. God is waiting on me to allow him to come in and renew me from the inside out. Ah'Lee loved me and always forgave me. He never left my side. He loved me unconditionally and when I saw the movie, it made me think about the love God has for me. If Ah'Lee loved me that much I can't imagine the love for me that God has. I love him and trust him. From this day forward I will keep my eyes on the Father, Son, and the holy spirit. I may get off track because of my flesh but I will do my best to remember to go back to God because he will never let anything take me down because he loves me. I may feel empty now but God is allowing me to feel this way so he can come in and make my heart whole again. I'm excited!!

I love you, my Buddy. Goodnight Baby!!

Journal Entry: 4-6-17

Tanika K. Judie

Buddy, we need to talk. What's up with these chicks you was supposed to be messing with? Buddy, you was cheating on me? If so, which I think you was based off our cousin, inbox's momma and sister was getting. That sh*t don't feel good at all. I'm trying not to be mad, but I don't get why you would do that to me. Then you had a hickey on yo neck that you said wasn't now I think or know it was now. One of them chicks caught you slipping like I told you. They wanted me to know. On one of the drunk, sloppy drunk nights you got caught sleep or something. I don't appreciate that sh*t at all Ah'Lee!! Even though you are gone that sh*t still hurts my heart. You told me you loved me and couldn't leave me but you was out here f***ing CHICKS. That's f***ed up. It's good though. I'm keeping my last name because I don't wanna look stupid. Being yo wife and side chicks laughing at me. I can't believe you. It's good though. I had to get that out. Love you

4-7-17

God please help me feel better I've been trying but nothing is working, why not? I need you now, I need the Father, the Son and the Holy Spirit to help me. I can't and am not willing to do this alone. I'm tired, I can't do this without you. I don't want to shut down but I feel myself slowly shifting. Jesus where are you please come talk to me. Fill me with the Holy Spirit. I am so broken!! God I need you to fix me. I understand it won't happen overnight but if you give me something saying you are here I know it would help me in some way. I wanna start you Bo waking me up for my children. I really do. I don't know where they would go if I didn't wake up but I'm tired. I would rather sleep than deal with this torture daily. After they go to school I would rather sleep until they come home make they are good and go back to sleep dwells !!! I know if I say your Name or "just" your name its a prayer! You know what I me need!! Help me Jesus, Lord have Mercy on me, heal my broken heart, put me back together and make me whole again. Please you !! I feel horrible Lord God why can't I see him in my dreams? Why hasn't he come talk to me? Is he mad at me still? If I would have stayed would I be better and he be okay and be here still Was that really his date to leave earth? I should have stayed he would have been home I shouldn't have left him like that I keep hearing voices and about what he told us and I loved him but I think I hurt him if you look. Yesterday twp afternoon I'm upset. We could have changed our hearts and we could have went our seperate ways but you didn't you allowed us to stay together but why. if

Tanika K. Judie

God, please help me feel better. I've been trying but nothing is working. Why not? I need you now. I need the father, the son and the holy spirit to help me. I can't and am not willing to do this alone. I'm tired, I can't do this without you. I don't want to shut down, but I feel myself slowly slipping. Jesus where are you please come talk to me. Fill me with the holy spirit. I am so broken!! God, I need you to fix me. I understand it won't happen overnight but if you give me something saying you are here, I know it would help me in some way. I wanna thank you for waking me up for my children. I really do, I don't know what they would do if I didn't wake up but I'm tired. I would rather sleep than deal with this torture daily. After they go to school I would rather sleep until they come home to make sure they are good then go back to sleep. Jesus!! I know if I say your name or call your name it's prayer! You know what I need!! Help me, Jesus, Lord have mercy on me, heal my broken heart, put me back together and make me whole again. Please, Jesus!! I feel horrible. And God why can't I see him in my dream? Why hasn't he come talk to me? Is he mad at me still? If I would have stayed would I be better, and would he be okay and still be here? Was that really his date to leave earth? I should have stayed he would have been home. I shouldn't have left him like that. I know he was sad about that. He loved us and I loved him but I think I hurt him. If you took him to get my attention I'm upset. You could have changed our hearts and we could have went our separate ways but you didn't you allowed us to stay together but why if

you where going to just take him away from us
physically? Why God why? I know you allow things
to happen but why this? Why do you think I can
handle this God why? I don't understand any of this
or why you even want me help me understand
God. Where is Jesus! Where is he God! I have
need him. He knows this and so do you so where
are you? Do I need to have a near death experience
to see and talk to all of you? I'm a mess God help
me! Please help me! I love you God I still honor your
name and your son! I praise you for what you will
do for me eventually but I need to know what's for
you to come. Lord lead me guide me go with and in
by me oh Lord I pray each day with faith in your
son Jesus name, Amen !! P.S. Please help me!!

God- Good morning Devin, I love you and miss you. If I
could do this over again with you I would. I would do
some things different but I still would lead you the
right way I wouldn't dwell on small things. I would
let them go and love on you and give you a little
more time to receive them without haunting you
to understand and change them over night. I know that
over somethings I did that weren't right somethings we
said to each other were very hurtful but I realize that
I pray you forgive me because I forgive you. I wish I
could tell you that. I wish we could talk and I hear your
voice talking back. I hate this and I don't understand. I
wish you and Jesus could come explain it to me. Well...
I love you and we all miss you God rest home. Love ya Devin!!

you were going to just take him away from us physically? Why God Why? I know you allow things to happen but why this? Why do you think I can handle this God why? I don't understand any of this or why you even want me. Help me understand God. Where is Jesus? Where is he, God! I need him! He knows this and so do you so where are you. Do I need to have a near-death experience to see and talk to all of you? I'm a mess God help me! Please Help me! I love you and I still honor your name and your son! I praise you for what you will do for me eventually, but I need to know what to do for you to come. Lord, lead me guide me go with me and stand by me oh Lord I pray each day with thee. In your son Jesus name, AMEN!! P.S. Please Help Me!!

Good morning Ah'Lee, I love you and miss you. If I could do this over again with you I would. I would do some things differently, but I still would lead you the right way. I wouldn't dwell on small things. I would let them go and love on you and give you a little more time to receive them without hounding you to understand and change them overnight. I know there are some things I did that weren't right. Some things we said to each other were very hurtful, but I apologize, and I pray you forgive me because I forgive you. I wish I could tell you that. I wish we could talk, and I hear your voice talking back. I hate this and I don't understand. I wish you and Jesus could come to explain it to me. Well, I love you and we all miss you. Until next time. Love you, my Buddy!!

I miss you so much my Buddy." Some days are good or I'll say better then other days but damn this is hard. I hate coming home without you. I've always been nervous about you leaving me. If figured if anybody was going to leave it would be me leaving you because I felt like you just didn't do it. Then Velma home and you are gone for good and not in a way I ever wanted you to leave me. I ent belief I have to live without you here on earth with me. Please come talk to me in my dream or something please I need you Baby. I love you so much and I'm still in love with you. Please don't forget about me Buddy. Please come to me I'm begging. I need to hear from you. I love you again! Your Wife Tonita Blackmon

4-8-17

Good morning God and Buddy. I love you with everything I have in me God. Buddy I love you so much and miss you. Today I'm getting out their house me and the kid's are going to Ro house. She has been out town with the Rob all week so we are going over their. Buddy, I rode around with Fovia, Harjah and Alexis last night we had a good time. We really enjoyed our selves. Just being with them made me feel great. The only thing was I had to come home and you wasn't here and I knew you wasn't going to be on your days. Saw my friend Steph. But I can't talk to him no more because he doesn't respect what I'm going though. I hate that. Why can't we just be helle too? When

I miss you so much, my Buddy!! Some days are good, or I'll say better than other days but damn this is hard. I hate coming home without you. I was always been nervous about you leaving me. I figured if anybody was going to leave it would be me leaving you because I felt like you just didn't get it. Then I come home, and you are gone for good and not in a way I ever wanted you to leave me. I can't believe I have to live without you here on earth with me. Please come talk to me in my dream or something please. I need you baby. I love you so much and I'm still in love with you. Please don't forget about me, Buddy. Please come to me I'm begging. I need to hear from you. I love you again! Your wife
Tamika Johnson

Journal Entry: 4-8-17

Good morning God and Buddy, I love you with everything I have in me, God. Buddy, I love you so much and miss you. Today I'm getting out this house me and the kids are going to Ro house. She has been out of town with the kids all week. So, we are going over there. Buddy, I rode around with your sister, your cousin and her friend last night we had a good time. We really enjoyed ourselves. Just being with them made me feel good. The only thing was I had to come home and you wasn't here and I knew you wasn't going to be on your way. Saw my friend but I can't talk to him anymore because he doesn't respect what I'm going through. I hate that. Wy can't we just be real cool. When

I'm sad, I can count on him to be a cool listening ear but my Buddy are clowns. I'm sad, hurt, and pissed. Missing you Buddy. However, I'm not desperate. I'm cool on niggas I'm focused on God and getting myself together. & anybody has a problem with that they can move the fuck around. Well my Buddy I miss you every second of the day and I love you and I'm still in love with you & that the thought of another woman having what could or what was mine make me mad. I hope you weren't out here fucking on a bunch of bitches. It'll not even one bitch. It hurts my feelings even thinking about it. I love you and made you but if I ever find out or have proof that you cheated or was cheating on me I'm going to pray that God changes my anger towards you. Because it just ain't ain't cheating. And, I love you and I'm waiting on you to deliver me and rescue me from this hole I'm falling into. I love you again! Baby I mean!

4-9-17

God, I thank you!! I thank you for your son Jesus! I thank you for understanding. Not saying my journey will be easy but it was all a part of your plan for my life. You have a unique way of designing this to line up for your purpose and so you will get the glory. Father I thank you for Rayven and her Man. I thank you to bring them to speak to me. I was searching for you and I had you this whole time. God I thank you. I thought I didn't know what makes me happy but I do and that's speaking to and

Tanika K. Judie

I'm sad, I can count on him to be cool listening ear but no. Dudes are clowns. I'm sad, hurt and missing you Buddy. However, I'm not desperate. I'm cool on people I'm focused on God and getting myself together. If anybody has a problem with that they can move around. Well, my Buddy, I miss you every second of the day and I love you and I'm still in love with you. Oh, but the thought of another woman having what (you) or what was mine makes me mad. I hope you wasn't out here messing with a bunch of chicks. Hell, not even one chick. It hurts my feelings even thinking about it. I love you and miss you but if I ever find out or have proof that you cheated or was cheating on me I'm going to have to pray that God changes my anger towards you because if not right back ain't cheating. God, I love you and I'm waiting on you to deliver me and rescue me from this hole I'm falling into. I love you again! Buddy, I miss you!

Journal Entry: 4-9-17

God, I thank you!! I thank you for your son, Jesus! I thank you for understanding. Not saying my journey will be easy but it was all part of your plan for my life. You have a unique way of designing this to line up for your purpose and so you will get the glory. Father, I thank you for Rayva and Man Man. I thank you for using them to speak to me. I was searching for you and I had you the whole time. God, I thank you. I thought I didn't know what makes me happy, but I do and that's speaking to and

encouraging people on all levels. Even in my time of pain and test you put something in me that lights up and gives me what I need to help someone else. God, you are amazing. You reveal a lot of things to me today. Thank God, thank you, Jesus! I thank you in advance. To be set apart means that I am apart from anything that is not of you or doesn't have you in it. Buddy left because he had to, and I don't have to hold on to anything that

Tanika K. Judie

is connected to him. I can slowly back up before I fall in to deep. I need to be with you and mend some relationships that have been keeping me bound. Lord, I wanna be free from the yoke of slavery. Buddy is set free, so I am free as well. I was told he kept me from certain things and people for a reason. So, I'm not going to keep holding on to those things. I can still keep in touch, but I will not be a part of anything. I can love on people from a distance and still be ok and do my part. I will live and not die. Lord, I thank you for allowing me to feel this pain I've never felt before so I would know to not go there again. Nothing or nobody comes before you!! You are the Great I Am, and I submit to you, Lord! I thank you for where I am right now, and I will move and do what you want me to do as you tell me to. I am nothing and can do nothing without you! And I thank you for that God. I don't wanna do anything without you, God. Please forgive me for my sin and sinful ways. I love you and thank you for grace, mercy, faith, joy, and love!! In Jesus name, Amen!!

BUDDY, I NEED YOU HERE WITH ME!!
God please I need you more then anything!
Please come and help me. Jesus please!!

Is there an address to heaven heaven? I need to send a few letters. If only we could send letters to heaven from earth.

Buddy, I miss you so much. I wish you was here with me. I can't believe this is my reality. why me? why us? we all love you and miss you. We miss your talk, your smile, your laugh, and even you eating up all the snacks from us. I never thought knew I could miss you this much. You. you here one day sleeping with me and the next day I'm alone. I love the way you held me the last 2 nights. bed with you it was simply amazing. I miss you baby. I be telling myself you will be back soon. I can't believe this is real we loved each other so much. I still love you! I'm still going to celebrate our living on our wedding or the day we planned to get married. I went today and picked out my mommy food and I wanted it feels like we are planning our wedding the one missing is you baby. I want to see you and talk to you. I feel so alone without you. no one or nothing can make me feel the way you did. Your touch was amazing. I've never felt the way I felt with you with anyone else. My baby, my husband. Damn. I miss you. I want you to know I love you to life. You will always hold a special place in my heart. You are the love of my life. And I'm still in love with you.

Tanika K. Judie

BUDDY, I NEED YOU HERE WITH ME!! God please I need you more than anything! Please come and help me. Jesus Please!!

Is there an address to heaven? I need to send a few letters. If only we could send letters to heaven from earth.

Buddy, I miss you so much. I wish you was here with me. I can't believe this is my reality. Why me? Why us? We all love you and miss you. We miss your face, your smile, your laugh, and even you eating up all the snacks from us. I never knew I would miss you this much. You were here one day sleeping with me and the next day I'm alone. I love the way you held me the last 2 nights I had with you. It was simply amazing. I miss you baby. I be telling myself you will be back soon. I can't believe this is real. We loved each other so much. I still love you! I'm still going to celebrate our union on our wedding day, well the day we planned to get married. I went today and picked out what momma, Tasha and I wanted. It feels like we are planning our wedding the one missing is you baby. I want to see you and talk to you. I feel so alone without you no one or nothing can make me feel the way you did. Your touch was amazing. I've never felt the way I felt with you with anyone else. My baby, my husband. Damn, I miss you. I want you to know I love you to life. You will always have a special place in my heart. You are the love of my life. And I'm still in love with you! I love you, my Buddy!!

I miss you so much, my Buddy! I love you even more! Wishing I could feel your touch. Missing you!!

I miss you my Buddy, I wish you were here, and our lives could go back to normal. I'm trying to get a grip of everything but it's a little overwhelming. I'm so used to you being here it's hard to get used to you being gone. I hate this s**t!! I love you, my Buddy!!

Are there human angels on earth from God? If so, can these angels lose their way and get off track once they are in the flesh? I believe in angels, but I *wonder if angels on earth is a thing. I'm going to ask. I know God sent his son Jesus in human flesh, but he never strayed from his father. Can angels be on earth from God, lose their way and find it again? Hhmmmm......?? If so, I think Ah'Lee was an angel and so was I. I lost my way God sent Ah'Lee (an angel) to help me find it. In the midst, he lost his way and I helped him find it. Once he found it God took him home because the flesh is a dangerous shell. So, he called back his angel!! He wasn't strong enough to be on earth and stay focused. He cared about people to much and often got distracted.*

Goodnight my Buddy and God!! I love you so much. Buddy, I miss you and I love you like crazy. Still waiting to talk to you in my dreams but I know you will come when the time is right. I love you again baby!! Missing him so much!!

Buddy, I love you and miss you so much! I feel like I can't do this, I want you with us Bud!! I don't understand this but this pain is horrible, it hurts physically. I don't want this pain why won't God come down and help me. Hold me and let me know it's going to be okay! Come down down and hold my hand and tell me what to do to get through this. I don't want this pain. I miss you so much!! WHERE ARE YOU God? You told me you will be here for me, you told me to trust you and I have. I've had faith in you so where are you? What do I need to do? TELL ME GOD!! I'm so mad at you God!! Why did you take him, why did you do this to me? Why did you leave me like this God? What am I supposed to do now God! HELP ME GOD PLEASE!! ---

Tanika K. Judie

Buddy, I love you and miss you so much! I feel like I can't do this. I want you with us bad!! I don't understand this s**t. This pain is horrible, it hurts physically. I don't want this pain. Why won't God come down and help me? Hold me and let me know it's going to be okay! Come down and hold my hand and tell me what to do to get through this. I don't want this pain. I miss you so much!! WHERE ARE YOU, GOD? You told me you will be here for me, you told m to trust you and I have. I've had faith in you so, where are you? What do I need to do? TELL ME, GOD!! I'm so mad at you God!! Why did you do this to me? Why did you leave me like this God? What am I sup-posed to do now God? HELP ME GOD PLEASE!!

PLEASE, GOD, HELP ME PLEASE GOD, I NEED YOU NOW GOD. I CAN'T DO THIS WITHOUT YOU I CAN'T DO ANYTHING WITHOUT You God. I don't wanna do this, I don't wanna feel this pain. I'm BROKEN, GOD!! I wanna sleep my day away God! I need to be okay for my kids but what do I do if I'm no good for myself GOD? WHAT DO I DO?? I'm so tired of feeling all this pain in my life GOD it's too much hurt and pain dang near all my life, GOD!! Please send the HOLY SPIRIT down and help me. I'm TIRED GOD! This pain feels unbearable. I thought you said you wouldn't put more on us then we can bare, so why did you give me something that is unbearable to me? Everything I love gets snatched, snatched away from me. Why couldn't he be here and be on his own? Not away for good God. Why did you do this? I know there is a birth date and a death date, but God was this really his date? I've been telling myself it was so I can feel better and convince myself that it was his death date and no matter if he got shot or not, he was going to pass away on that day. Is that true God. If not, why wouldn't you stop it? Why would you let him die? I know he's in heaven with you but what about us God? What do we do? And not just us but his other family members especially his mother and his daughters? What am I going to to do for the baby if I'm messed up myself? How can I help any of our children God how?? I need you God please help me, God! Please, I'm begging you, God!!

Tanika K. Judie

PLEASE!!

NOTE: *I felt like I was losing my mind. I remember begging God to help me because I was so tired of feeling the physical pain from losing my Buddy! I was devasted, broken, torn, angry, lost, confused, and suicidal. I wanted to say forget it all, but I knew my kids needed me. I can't say that I didn't try but God wasn't having it. I was so mad at God but acting as if I wasn't just so he would help me. If you have ever felt this way just know you are not alone, and you are not losing your mind. Keep praying and NEVER stop! Yell, scream and talk to God because he hears all your cries.*

Share Your Thoughts.......

20. EMOTIONAL ROLLER COASTER

After all that writing, praying, screaming, and crying out to God, I still wasn't okay. Utterly devastated, I didn't know what to do. With all the stress and lack of sleep, I started having seizures back to back and ended up in my neurologist's office. We needed to come up with a plan because my medication wasn't working. Soon after arriving at her office, I gave her the news: she hadn't heard anything about the tragic, life-changing turn of events.

We cried together and discussed treatment options. She confirmed that my extremely high-stress level was impeding the medication's ability to work. These stress-induced seizures were not caused by Epilepsy, however; they were non-epileptic seizures. The only way to treat those, she advised, was to see a psychiatrist, who could help with the stress, depression, and grieving process. Of course, I was hesitant but knew she was right; and I also couldn't go back to work until my seizures were under control. I trusted my doctor and knew that she wanted the best for me.

We talked about where to go to seek treatment, and she recommended Research Psychiatric. That was a good choice, but only if they had an out-patient option as I didn't want to leave my children and stay there.

"Yes, they do have outpatient," she said.

I said, "Okay," made a follow-up appointment, and left.

I sat outside in the car and cried my eyes out.

While sitting there behind the wheel, thoughts of killing myself came flooding back. I just wanted to feel better, and I needed the pain to stop. But then I thought about my children—could I really leave them to continue on this earth alone? *"All my children have is me . . . I can't do that to them . . . they don't deserve that!"* My love for them won out over my self-doubt and despair.

Wiping my tears, I decided to call my job to let them know what the doctor had said; I also faxed them the paperwork to confirm that what I was saying was true. And then needing some encouragement, I called a friend ... We cried, and both agreed that it would be for the best. After lots more talking and tears, I told her I was about to go and do the intake if it wasn't too late. We hung up, and I headed toward the hospital, deciding not to tell the doctors that I was suicidal as I knew they would admit me.

Pulling up in front of the hospital, I said a prayer, something like, *"Dear Lord, please help me, and touch the people with wisdom and compassion; let them really help me and not just try to medicate me—because, Lord, I need more than medication."* After saying, "Amen," I took a deep breath and stepped out of the car.

Walking up to the building, I reached my hand out to grab the door but hesitated—I really didn't want to have to do this, but I needed some help. Cautiously grabbing the door handle, I walked in. The lobby was full of people, all staring at me—or so I thought. I felt so embarrassed, but I had to do it. I walked up to the desk and asked the receptionist, "Am I too late to do an intake?"

"No, ma'am, you're not," she replied.

"Okay," I said, "I'd like to speak to someone about doing an outpatient treatment."

"Of course, can I have your name?"

"Tamika Judie."

"Okay, Ms. Judie, I need you to complete these forms and bring them back up to me; then we will put you on the list."

"Okay, thank you," I said.

I turned around and found a seat. The forms had so many questions that I didn't want to answer because I didn't want to seem like I was really going crazy—so I lied just to make sure I wouldn't get admitted. After what seemed like forever, I completed the long forms and took them back to the receptionist. She looked them over to make sure I had completed everything, told me to have a seat, and said she would put me on the list.

The next thing I knew, my name was called. After following the intake specialist to the back, she asked me some of the same questions that I'd just answered on the form. Was I frustrated? Yes, and second-guessing myself, too, so I answered her questions with an attitude. She then looked at me and asked me to tell her in detail why I was there.

I swallowed hard, fought back tears, and begin to speak. I told her what happened, and she was empathetic, letting me know that she thought the outpatient treatment would be a good fit for me. She said I had to come every day though, from 8:00 a.m. to 3:00 p.m. I agreed to be there, we talked for a second, and then after we shook hands, I left. That night, I couldn't sleep because, again, everything was assaulting my mind, including the inevitability of going to the crazy place (as I called it) the next day. I wasn't ready, but it had to be done.

The next morning, after getting my children up and off to school, I got in the car and headed down to the hospital; I knew I had to get it over with, so I put on my big girl panties and walked right up to the front desk, checked in, and waited to be let in the back. After only a minute or two, I was told to come through a door next to the front desk. Yes, I was super nervous, but I walked over to the door, pulled the handle, and walked in....

This was the first day of what I thought would be my healing. Yet, I was sadly mistaken. It was the first day of me facing reality, which only made things worse.

STAY TUNED IN FOR

Pain into Purpose:
Facing Reality while Rebuilding This Thing Called Life

5 STAGES OF GRIEF

Denial: *The action of declaring something to be untrue. Denial helps us to reduce the pain of loss. You are running from the truth trying to disconnect what is real and what's not. Denial in grief is not accepting or facing reality, it allows us to act as the loss didn't happen.*

Anger: *A strong feeling of annoyance, displeasure, or hostility. This anger can be towards anybody; strangers, friends or family members and even your own children. You will even be angry at the person or thing that you lost. You try to find something or someone to be mad at or blame for the loss because it feels better to lash out because you don't know any other way to deal with it. Anger is like an emotional outlet when you are grieving. It allows us to express ourselves without being judged or caring what someone thinks.*

Bargaining: *Negotiate the terms and conditions of a transaction. When you are in this stage you may feel desperate and are willing to do anything or give anything to cope with the loss and to be in less pain. You try to reason with God or anybody to feel better even if that means putting yourself at risk or in danger to feel less pain. I.E. "I will do better if you will* *give it him/her/it back to me." "God, if you do this for me I will never sin again." You search for your own faults, mistakes, and shortcomings that you feel may have caused this to happen and try to reason with something to reverse what happen.*

Depression: *A serious condition that can lead to an inability to function or suicide. Depression can cause a downward spiral of emotions which in turn can cause you to do things that can hurt you emotionally and physically. Depression in grief is the most common and the most dangerous. You become consumed with sadness and no matter what you do nothing makes you feel better. Depression looks different or can be different for every individual person, but it is very real. This happens when we finally calm down and start to slowly process the reality of the situation. This happens when we start to face the fact that what we have experienced is real and there is not changing it or waking up because what we thought was a dream was not, but it was very real. The other stage has passed, there is not more denial at this time, there is no shock/ denial, there is only the hard truth that we must face. I will say that there is no time limit on how long you go through each stage or how many times you go back and forth between each one. You can go from 1 to 2 or 2 to 4 or it can start at 4 or 5 and then the other stages. In this stage, we disconnect from the world in a way. We feel alone and sometimes it gets so bad that the pain is not just on the inside, but it is becoming a physical pain that hurts and it hurts so bad that you may want to end it all. I hate this stage and the people that have been through this or is going through this I am in praying for you. I want you to know that it gets better as time goes on so stay strong, pray and trust that God will carry you out of this stage.*

Acceptance: the act of assenting or believing. This stage I haven't mastered yet, I go back and forth with it. However, it is acknowledging and believing that the situation or loss that took place is ok. You learn to live with the truth. This doesn't mean you forget that person or thing that you lost but you learn to function and live life without it and without going through the 4 stages listed above. It's like you finally allow yourself to be free from the pain and overwhelming sadness that you felt every time you thought about the person/thing you lost. I also like to think that you finally allow that person or thing to be free as well. Acceptance releases you from the bondage and lifts the weight you once carried from the loss. Acceptance is when you can really be happy and live again. Wait, you may at times experience some sadness and regret but the emotional roller coaster you go through with the other stages are less likely.

◆ ◆ ◆

Although people grieve differently, we all go through these 5 stages of grief. Sometimes in a different order and sometimes people stay in one stage longer than the other but if we understand what is happening then we can learn what each emotion is that we are feeling. And at that time, we can find some comfort in knowing that we are just going through the process.

SEEK HELP

Listed below are resources you can use if you are experiencing any of the things listed below.

Don't be afraid to get help.

- Suicide Prevention Lifeline (24/7 Telephone number): 1-800-273-8255 or 1-800-784-2433
- Suicide.org: Suicide Prevention, Awareness, and support
- Crisis Text Line (24/7): Text – HOME to 741741
- Feeling Depressed or not yourself contact your nearest doctor and or mental health specialist.

For more information on resources for help go to www.herofficially.simplesite.com

IN LOVING MEMORY OF....

Dorron Lee Blackmon
3/24/1985 – 3/11/2017

PAIN INTO PURPOSE